A CAPTIVE NO MORE

Finding the Life God Has Planned for You

MARK KILLINGSWORTH

CROSSBOOKS

CrossBooks™
A Division of LifeWay
One LifeWay Plaza
Nashville, TN 37234
www.crossbooks.com
Phone: 1-866-768-9010

First published by CrossBooks 07/31/2014

ISBN: 978-1-4627-3823-6 (sc)
ISBN: 978-1-4627-3825-0 (hc)
ISBN: 978-1-4627-3824-3 (e)

Library of Congress Control Number: 2014910284

Printed in the United States of America.

This book is printed on acid-free paper.

Special Appreciation

I want to give special attention and appreciation to some very important people in my life who have helped me greatly with this book. Vickie Killingsworth, Aaron Killingsworth, Callie Newton, Arie Carter, Stephanie Dalla Rosa, Michael Haynes and my brother Scotty Killingsworth all gave significant help in the editing and development. They each have given hours to this project providing their skill, wisdom and insights on how to improve this material.

I want to thank the Stonebridge Church of Nixa, Missouri, for their support, especially the small groups that helped me walk through this book. This process helped to create the Leader's Guide that is a tool for small group leaders.

I want to show appreciation to Nathan Colba for his great work in the graphic art production on the cover of this book. If you have need of effective graphic art, you can contact Nathan at www.baselinemedia.com.

Special Thanks

MY FAMILY: The writing of a book is a time consuming and challenging proposition. It would have been impossible to accomplish if not for the support and encouragement of my wife Vickie, and our children: Aaron, Sean and wife Shaunda, Ashley and husband Brandon, Kurt and wife Katie, and Brett. These are the loves of my life and the support system that has helped me through my own journey from being **a captive no more**.

MY CHURCH: I am grateful for Elders and a church family that allowed me the opportunity to learn the principles of this story and gave me the time to organize my thoughts to be presented in this book. I am blessed to be a member of this great family of God.

Special Dedication

My parents, Lon and Maxine Killingsworth, skillfully helped me and my brothers avoid many of the bondages that bring great destruction on people's lives. Because of their love, faith, and lives, my brothers Scotty, Gary, Lonnie, and myself have been greatly blessed by this Godly heritage. I would like to dedicate this book in memory of my father, who went to be with the Lord in July of 2011.

Contents

Introduction

I am writing this introduction at a time when many things look bleak for America. We are ten years into an unpopular war in Iraq, Russia has just overtaken Crimea with the threat of greater advancement, the national debt continues to grow at a staggering rate leading to a predictable financial collapse, our government seems to be heading headlong into socialism which is a cancer to the American experiment, and an underlying hopelessness seems to be growing in the American culture.

We are facing a growing division in the vision of our country. One group to the Right side of the spectrum wants to hold on to conservatism, a free-market, business-based economy, a foundation of truth focused on the teachings of Jesus Christ, and a vision of America as the nation that is a hope and light to the world. The other group on the Left side of the spectrum wants an America where the government is responsible for taking care of its people, truth is subjective, and personal freedom is the philosophy of belief.

Many are crying out that catastrophe is coming. The *right side* is warning the nation that unless we wake up and turn back to the principles of God's Word - judgment is coming. The *left side* is pushing steadily forward an agenda that seems to move our nation further and further toward an antichrist future. Is there any hope for America?

I encourage you to use this book as a workbook. You will find questions that hopefully will help you process steps to freedom in your own life.

In this book I would like to hold a torch up high with a light for a path that would lead you personally from a place of bondage toward a life of abundance. If enough people caught a glimpse of the light, maybe—just maybe—America could once again become a nation with a bright vision.

Join me in this journey, "A CAPTIVE NO MORE."

SECTION #1

Understanding Bondage

CHAPTER 1

"Understanding Bondage"

The New York Times headline read, "Jaycee Dugard's 'Stolen Life': 18 Years of Abuse." This horrible event occurred on June 10, 1991, in South Lake Tahoe, California. Jaycee Lee was 11 years old at the time she was abducted from a street near her home while walking to the school bus stop, an action taken by thousands of kids each day. But on this day, for this young lady, an eighteen-year nightmare of bondage began. The article tells us that "hers is a story of her being yanked out of her normal life at the age of 11; spending 18 years imprisoned by the convicted rapist, Phillip Garrido and his wife, Nancy; and bearing two daughters by Mr. Garrido."

A lead was found on August 24, 2009, when Garrido visited the campus of UC Berkeley accompanied by two young girls that showed signs of extreme nervousness and social awkwardness. As people observed the unusual behavior of the girls, they reported their observations to local police. Their report sparked an investigation that led Garrido to bring the two girls to a parole office a couple days later, accompanied by a young woman who was then identified as Jaycee Lee Dugard.

On April 28, 2011, Garrido and his wife were arrested for kidnapping and other charges. At their trial, they pleaded guilty to Dugard's kidnapping, which included 18 years of bondage and sexual assault.

As the trial information began to be released to the public, it was stated that "law enforcement officers believe Jaycee Lee was kept in a concealed area behind Garrido's house in Antioch, California for 18 years. …During this 18 year period of confinement, Jaycee Lee bore two daughters fathered by Garrido, who were aged 11 and 15 at the time of her reappearance."

Having not experienced anything remotely close to what Jaycee Lee experienced, I find it difficult to comprehend all of the terrors and levels of pain that she must have experienced under physical and emotional bondage from a madman. I find it difficult to have any sense of mercy for a person like Garrido—a man who is so perverted in his soul that he is capable of bringing this type of evil on others.

As much as we hate it, this kind of atrocity happens. The reality is such that bondage has its evil grip on people at various levels all around us every day.

Bondage is a condition of servitude to someone or something that has no power to offer freedom.

The result is a hopeless and powerless life hindered from finding the greatness that God designed for each person. The reality that there may be severe or even small levels of bondage in our life should motivate us to seek God's plan for deliverance.

With a little time and effort to get to know the people around us, we will begin to see bondages that may be robbing people of their God-given lives.

Billy can't stop drinking. Staying numb to the pain of his bondage consumes his thoughts and has become the goal he pursues.

Sherry is now in prison because her drive to gamble led her to embezzle thousands of dollars from her job to cover gambling losses.

James is now divorced and separated from his wife, his children, and his home because of his addiction to pornography. The easy and quick self-gratification led to an unfaithfulness that destroyed his family.

Jennifer was so lost and felt such emptiness inside that she lost control of her health. Food became her guilty obsession, and now she is bed-ridden with diseases that are destroying her body because her weight is over 400 pounds.

The once vivacious Melody is now in a personal bondage of fear. The feeling of fear has grown so powerful that she now relies on Prozac to stabilize her emotions enough that she can even get out of bed in the morning.

The United States of America, a nation who once had a vision to be a light set on a hill and a beacon of hope, is now in a moral and financial bondage that is leading to bankruptcy and a moral decline.

...on and on the stories go. Is there any hope?

Is there a way back from our bondages?

Is there a path of truth that, with determined faith, we could take to re-emerge from our pit?

What is bondage?

After this reading, you may be able to identify some of the bondages that are keeping friends and family from experiencing full life in Jesus Christ.

Name some of the bondages you can see in others.

Let's begin an investigation to see if there is a way out of our bondages so that we might find the life designed for us by God Himself.

An Old Story

Our search for answers will begin at the beginning of recorded history in the book of Genesis, one of the oldest stories ever told. Genesis is part of the Pentateuch, the foundational scriptures of the Jewish nation, better known to us as the first five books of the Holy Bible. This is the story of a people chosen by God to be His representatives to the world. They were a people with value, vision, and a God-given purpose. They were a people with a promise from God. The promise to Abraham, the patriarch of the Jewish nation, was recorded as follows:

> *I will make you a great nation and I will bless you; I will make your name great, and you will be a blessing. I will bless those who bless you, and whoever curses you I will curse; and all peoples on earth will be blessed through you.*

> (Genesis 12:2–4 NIV)

The Jews lost their way and became disconnected from the vision and promise God had given their forefather Abraham. In the same way, America has lost her way and become disconnected from the vision of her forefathers.

The book of Exodus opens up with a tale of how the Jewish people lost their way and found themselves far from the promise God had given to Abraham. This was the beginning of their bondage. Let's look at the passage below:

> *Then Joseph died, and all his brothers and all that generation. But the people of Israel were fruitful and increased greatly; they multiplied and grew exceedingly strong, so that the land was filled with them.*

> *Pharaoh Oppresses Israel*

> *Now there arose a new king over Egypt, who did not know Joseph. And he said to his people, "Behold, the people of Israel are too many and too mighty for us. Come, let us deal shrewdly with them, lest they multiply, and, if war breaks out, they join our enemies and fight against us and escape from the land." Therefore, they set taskmasters over them to afflict them with heavy burdens. They built for Pharaoh store cities, Pithom and Raamses. But the more they were oppressed, the more they multiplied and the more they spread*

abroad. And the Egyptians were in dread of the people of Israel. So they ruthlessly made the people of Israel work as slaves and made their lives bitter with hard service, in mortar and brick, and in all kinds of work in the field. In all their work they ruthlessly made them work as slaves. (Exodus 1:6–14 ESV)

There are clues in this passage to help us identify the steps leading to bondage in our own lives.

1. **Losing Vision**
   "Now Joseph and all his brothers and all that generation died." (Exodus 1:6 ESV) There is a danger that grows as we get further from the original vision of faith that our forefathers developed from the truths of Scripture. The distance of space or time allows a drift from one generation to the next—a drift which has a natural undercurrent away from the foundations of truth. This is why God spoke to Moses about the importance of carefully and consistently teaching our children about the truths of God and His mighty works that He has done for His people.

   > *And these words that I command you today shall be on your heart. You shall teach them diligently to your children, and shall talk of them when you sit in your house, and when you walk by the way, and when you lie down, and when you rise. You shall bind them as a sign on your hand, and they shall be as frontlets between your eyes. You shall write them on the doorposts of your house and on your gates.* (Deuteronomy 6:6-9 ESV)

The danger is in losing the truth, vision, purpose, and character necessary to carry on God-given dreams.

2. **Complacency in Prosperity**
   Men who walked closely with God formulated the original vision. This vision was maintained by the sacrifice of many who gave their lives in order to secure the way for the vision to grow warring against corrosive

opposition. But as the vision became a reality there began to flow the blessings of prosperity that accompany obedience to the Lord. There is a hidden danger that can creep in during a time of prosperity. That danger is in becoming complacent.

Read Deuteronomy 28:1–14

With these blessings, our natural reaction is often to relax the efforts that protect the principles of the vision. This let-down allows complacency to set in. With complacency comes a further slacking of the effort that is necessary to maintain freedom.

3. **Selfishness Creates Room for the Enemy**

   As complacency increases, selfishness becomes more powerful and allows for a deceptive, dominating force to come in and take over. For example, Exodus 1:11 NIV says, "So they put slave masters over them to oppress them with forced labor, and they built Pithom and Rameses as store cities for Pharaoh." This happened to Israel again when Babylon was used by God to discipline His people for their selfishness by taking them into 70 years of captivity. It happened to the Roman Empire as well. The following issues have been identified as some of the causes of her failure: decline in morals, political corruption, failing economy, unemployment, and decline of ethics and values. As we compare these issues to the United States of America, I believe it is a clear model of the same process that is happening in our nation.

4. **Freedom Dies and Slavery Ensues**

   As freedom dies and bondage gains control, the pain of a life of slavery becomes a reality.

   > *So the Egyptians came to dread the Israelites and worked them ruthlessly. They made their lives bitter with hard labor in brick and mortar and with all kinds of work in the fields; in all their hard labor the Egyptians used them ruthlessly.* (Exodus 1:12–14 NIV)

For Israel, freedom was lost to the Egyptians. For America, the freedom is lost to the philosophy of liberalism.

> *Modern American liberalism is a form of social liberalism developed from progressive ideals such as Theodore Roosevelt's New Nationalism, Woodrow Wilson's New Freedom, Franklin D. Roosevelt's New Deal, John F. Kennedy's New Frontier, and Lyndon Johnson's Great Society. It combines social liberalism and social progressivism with support for a welfare state and a mixed economy. American liberal causes include... abortion rights for women and government entitlements such as education and health care.* (Just A Word From The Left, Word Press)

From my perspective, it appears that at its core, it is anti-God and anti-truth. It seeks personal freedom in a system that can only bring further bondage because of the moral, financial, and political deceptions it is built upon. This same thing happens on a personal basis. As our self-absorption increases, we have no defense left against demonic enemies who come in under deception. Before we are even aware of the reality, we find ourselves in bondage.

Let's Talk or Think About It

- **As you look at America, what are some of the bondages you can see that are threatening to destroy the very vision of our founding fathers as they sought to establish a country based upon the truths found in the Holy Bible?**

- **On a personal level, can you identify areas of bondage in your own life that continually works to keep you defeated?**

Read Luke 4:14–21 and answer the following questions.

- In this passage Jesus quotes from Isaiah 61:1–3 and He then declares that He is the fulfillment of this prophecy. As you break this statement apart what does Jesus say that He came to do and is able to accomplish?

- If Jesus does these things in people's lives, then what would happen to the bondages that keep people in slavery and the death that it brings?

CHAPTER 2

"A False Belief Is Planted"

The day starts like any other day. You wake up, get dressed, kiss your spouse goodbye, and go to work. But on this particular morning, the enemy of God's Kingdom will set in motion a plan to plant a seed in your heart and mind when you are unsuspecting. This seed thought may be planted in many different ways by a variety of people who hold a place of influence in your life. It can come in the form of a word curse, an abuse, a rejection, or an exposure to sin. Then, to make sure that the deception grows, Satan's messenger is sent to plant and water that seed thought that will take root for the ultimate purpose of a lifetime of mental and emotional bondage.

It happened like this for Mike.

Mike was raised in a military home. In other words, Dad was the commanding officer and everyone else in the family was to be an obedient soldier. Love and acceptance were seldom shared, and if there were actions of love or words of acceptance, they came only after one of the children showed extreme speed or overabundant obedience to the commander.

Obedience was not an option; it was demanded. Because anything less than perfection was accompanied by extreme punishment. These punishments would include latrine duty with tasks like scrubbing the bathroom floors with a toothbrush or kitchen duty with tasks like peeling potatoes, washing dishes, and cleaning the floor on your hands and knees with a brush. One of his dad's favorite forms of punishments, however, was a beating with a leather belt where Mike would have to lay on the bed with his bottom exposed. Of course, each of these punishments, when taken to the extreme, could plant an evil seed in the heart and mind of a child.

But for Mike, these were the easy punishments. The hard punishment came in his father's spoken word. Most often, Mike's father would add the words, **"You are a lazy son and you will never amount to anything."**

These words were burned into Mike's mind. His internal voice would play that message over and over on a continuous loop. This demonic seed was planted in the form of his father's message. It took root so deeply that everything Mike did and saw was through the lens his father had made: "You are a lazy son and you will never amount to anything."

This destructive "seed thought" that finds its way into a life is motivated by the demonic because the spirit and intent of the message is to damage the design of God in the life of a child.

At the end of Chapter 1 you were given an opportunity to write down your personal areas of bondage. Now I challenge you to take this one step further.

Using these questions below, attempt to find out when and where the bondage was planted in YOUR life.

What was the demonic lie that was planted in your life?

Who was used to plant the lie in your mind?

When was the lie started?

Where were you when this lie was planted?

Why do you think Satan wanted this lie planted in your life?

How has this planted lie affected your life?

In a later chapter we will discuss clear steps about how to remove this area of bondage in your life. But for now, we are only attempting to understand bondage and begin to identify the bondages that are keeping us from the full life that Jesus wants for us.

Read John 8:44 and John 10:10 and let's look at Satan's intent.

Many different people throughout your life can give a word curse to you. There is great power in words, especially when a person who has influence in our lives speaks them. That is why fathers, mothers, pastors, coaches, teachers, and bosses have such a huge impact on us. They have the power of life and death in their words.

There is a terrifying reality that we have the power to bless or to curse by the words we speak into other people's lives. The power to speak words of blessing comes from God's Kingdom. It is the Lord's desire that we agree with and speak God's design into people's lives. The power to curse comes from Satan's kingdom as we agree with and speak words that release death and destruction into a life. Words like these are used with the intent to hurt or hinder the design of God.

Paul said it like this in Scripture: *"For we do not wrestle against flesh and blood, but against principalities, against powers, against the rulers of the darkness of this age, against spiritual hosts of wickedness in the heavenly places."* (Ephesians 6:12 NKJV) In other words, we must be careful and intentional to speak words of life over those who fall under our care and in the same way be just as intentional never to allow our words to bring destruction to a person that God made and loves.

It is impossible for us to make it through our formative years without Satan's messenger getting through to us and planting a seed somewhere and somehow. We must be aware of this tactic and learn how to face the fact that we have had demonic seeds planted into our life and mind along the journey. There are probably some we are aware of and some that remain hidden. Either way, we all must find a way to dig out the seeds that have been planted in us. Unless we find victory over these spoken curses, those tiny seeds will eventually grow larger and larger until they are a great bondage, ultimately taking over our lives.

A curse can destroy us in any number of ways. A small word curse, left untreated, can lead to an addiction taken in an attempt to self-medicate and numb the pain. This is one reason we have so many people who are addicted in our society.

A curse can cause us to believe the deception and give up. The result is a wasted life that usually leaves a legacy of destruction on everyone it influences.

Mike's curse caused him to do the opposite of shutting down and giving up. Mike made a determination early in his life that he would live in such a way as to prove his dad's curse wrong.

This determination he made drove him like a slave master. He worked harder and longer than anyone else that surrounded his life. As a student, he studied harder; as an employee, he worked harder. As he pursued his career, he pushed harder than anyone else so that he could disprove the statement his father made, "You are a lazy son and you will never amount to anything."

No matter how well he did, Mike never felt it was good enough. His studies were never done to the level of his personal expectation, nor were his work ever accomplished enough to achieve his demand for perfection. No matter how high he rose in his career, it was never enough. With each effort, he would hear the voice of his father: "You are a lazy son and you will never amount to anything."

What did you learn about the power of words?

God knows the battles we all face in this life. He knows the obstructions that keep us slaves to failure. His plan for us is to provide a way of escape from our bondage. This is the plan that is revealed through the story of the Exodus.

Israel, God's people, represents you and me. Egypt represents bondage. In this story, Egypt decides to make the Israelites its slaves.

> *Therefore they set taskmasters over them to afflict them with heavy burdens. They built for Pharaoh store cities, Pithom and Raamses. But the more they were oppressed, the more they multiplied and the more they spread abroad. And the Egyptians were in dread of the people of Israel. So they ruthlessly made the people of Israel work as slaves.* (Exodus 1:11-14 ESV)

There are some important truths we can see from this example that will help us understand how bondage works.

- There is evil, Satan, whose intent is to enslave people by planting the deception that defines us as slaves.

- Satan places "slave masters" over us. These slave masters are the items that keep us in bondage, such as alcohol, drugs, pornography, critical spirit, depression, unbelief in God and His good news, wrong relationships, or abuse.

- The slave masters drive us to forced labor or servitude. This is where our bondage owns and defines us. We are no longer living as a child of God but a slave to an evil force.

- Once we are under a slave master, we find him ruthless. Ruthless is defined as having no pity: merciless, cruel.

Let's Talk or Think About It

As you read John 10:10-15, attempt to answer and discuss the following questions.

- **Who is the thief, and what is his purpose?**

- **Jesus identified Himself as the Good Shepherd. What is His purpose for your life?**

- **As the Good Shepherd, what does He do for us, His sheep?**

Mike is a friend of mine, and after I was separated from him for 20 years, we were able to spend some time together to get caught up. Mike is now in his mid-fifties, and the bondage in his life has taken a visible toll on his soul and body. He is 55 and looks 65. Is this because he is a bad guy? Absolutely not! He is a great guy. He has simply been enslaved to a message that was planted in his life as a youth, and the slave master has been ruthless.

Is this the only reality that we as humans have to look forward to? Later in this book, I will attempt to show that there is a real way to freedom and abundant living. But we need to truly understand what we are fighting against before we get to the answer of true life and true living.

John 10:10-15 identifies a clear warfare going on in the lives of all people. What feelings and thoughts do you have about this reality?

CHAPTER 3

"A Controlling Power Is Allowed"

As we discovered in the previous chapter, there is great power in the words that we speak, whether carelessly or intentionally. There are words that produce blessing and words that bring a curse. Scripture says that, *"The tongue has the power of life and death."* (Proverbs 18:21 NIV) Let's take a moment to see how this actually happens. There are three distinct steps:

1. Your words form an idea.
2. Those ideas assemble and create a belief.
3. Your beliefs drive your actions.

Let's try to walk through this process step by step by looking at this example. At the first of the year, you decide to attempt to lose weight by going on a diet. Three days into to your diet, hunger has raised its ugly head, and you crave large quantities of food.

Along comes a **WORD** in the form of an advertisement. "For a January special, we are offering you today a Big Mac Extra Value Meal with a chocolate shake for only $2.00."

Then that **WORD** starts to grow in your mind. You begin to figure that if you just skip dinner this evening and ride the stationary bike for 18 hours you can go ahead and get this meal. It is only $2.00, and you would be crazy not to do this. By this time, the initial **WORD** has become an **IDEA**.

That **IDEA** begins to develop further as you get the $2 out of your piggy bank. You get in your car and drive to the nearest McDonalds. On your drive to get that Big Mac you have rationalized why this has become a good idea. Excuses start coming to mind to reinforce the decision you are about to make. By this time the **IDEA** has become the **BELIEF** that you deserve a good meal. You argue that you can make up for it later. Then the belief results in **ACTION** and you find yourself sitting in the restaurant opening that white sack, pulling the lid off of that Big Mac Box, eating french fries from that big red container, and washing it all down with that thick... rich... chocolate... shake.

[Excuse me for a minute, I will continue with this story when I get back, but right now I am thinking about taking a little trip to McDonalds.]

I'm back and am now writing this next section while riding my stationary bike. Let's take a look at the progression again as to how a word spoken through suggestion grows into an idea that becomes a controlling thought pattern in our lives.

1. WORDS become IDEAS
2. IDEAS become BELIEF
3. BELIEF becomes ACTION

And this is exactly how a controlling thought becomes a power that drives our decisions.

Dylan Klebold and Eric Harris have become infamous names in American culture. These students were notorious for a killing rampage in a school in Columbine, Colorado. Their ACTION came from a BELIEF they had formed from an IDEA that was assembled. All of this came from a WORD that was spoken in their formative years. This word/thought developed into an IDEA that led to an unspeakable crime that has now been repeated in America several times.

The following is a journal entry written by Dylan Klebold before the massacre occurred in April of 1999 (http://acolumbinesite.com). The offensive language in this journal entry has been edited.

Ah yes, this is me writing... just writing, nobody technically did anything, just I felt like throwing out my thoughts - this is a weird time, weird life, weird existence. As I sit here (partially drunk w. a screwdriver) I think a lot. Think... Think... that's all my life is, just [edited] loads of thinking... all the time... my mind never stops... music runs 24/7 (xpt for sleep), just songs I hear, not necessarily good or bad, & thinking... about the [edited] in gym class, how he worries me, about driving, & my family, about friends & doings with them, about girls I know (mainly [edited] & [edited]), how I know I can never have them, yet I can still dream... I do [edited] to supposedly 'cleanse' myself in a spiritual, moral sort of way (deleting the 'limits' on my comp, not getting drunk for periods of time, trying not to ridicule/ make fun of people ([edited]) at school, yet it does nothing to help my life - morally. My existence is [edited]. To me - how I feel that I am in eternal suffering. In infinite directions in infinite realities - yet these [Dylan scribble] realities are fake- artificial, induced by thought, how everything connects, yet it's all so far apart.... & I sit & think... Science is the way to find solutions to everything, right? I still think that, yet I see different views of [edited] now like the mind - yet if the mind is viewed scientifically... HMM I dwell in the past... thinking of good & bad movies a lot on the past though... I've always had a thing for the past - how it reacts to the present & the future - or rather vice versa. I wonder how/ when I got so [edited] up... my mind, existence, problem - when Dylan Benet Klebold got covered up by this entity containing Dylan's body... as I see the people at school - some good, some bad - I see how different I am (aren't we all you'll say) yet I'm on such a greater scale of difference

> *(as far as I know, or guess) I see jocks having fun, friends, women. LIVES or rather shallow existences compared to mine (maybe). Like ignorance = bliss - they don't know this world (how I do in my mind or in reality, or in this existence) yet we each are lacking something that the other possesses -- I lack the true human nature that Dylan owned, & they lack the overdeveloped mind/ imagination/ knowledge tool I don't sit in here thinking of suicide gives me hope, that i'll be in my place wherever I go after this life. that ill finally not be at war w. myself, the world, the universe - my mind, body, everywhere, everything at PEACE... me- my soul (existence). & the routine - is still monotonous, go to school, be scared & nervous, somewhat hoping that people can accept me... that i can accept them... the NIN song Piggy is good for thought writing... The lost Highway sounds like a movie about me... I'm gonna write later, bye*

Within this journal entry you can see how WORDS became IDEAS and those IDEAS became BELIEFS that led to ACTIONS.

What are your thoughts and insights about Dylan Klebold that were revealed in his journal entry?

There are two particular sentences in Dylan's journal that catch my attention. The first is when Dylan talks about himself in the third person. "When Dylan got covered up by this entity containing Dylan's body." This seems to say that another entity had taken over the person who used to be Dylan. Then he described this new identity when he said, "I lack the true human nature that Dylan owned." At this point, Dylan saw himself as an evil entity.

The WORD curse Dylan heard was, "You are unacceptable and not worthy to be loved." (Although it is not clear from my research where this word curse was planted.)

Dylan developed the IDEA that he was not worthy to have a life of purpose and honor. It was in this vacuum that his weakness could be overtaken by a stronger power that he called "entity." This power, though dark and demonic, felt better to him than the emptiness of his cursed life. Then he described himself as having "no longer the human nature that I once had."

The BELIEF that developed from this idea was that there is no hope for the lost Dylan. There is no positive future available, therefore he felt the darkness called "entity" brought a power he had never experienced before.

The ACTION occurred when this new entity took revenge on those who had caused him to feel rejection. Then, to end the pain of his unacceptable existence, he killed himself.

This is how a controlling power of the demonic can gain full control in a life. The hope of the God-designed life is destroyed and replaced by an image of bondage that leads to hopelessness.

People may define themselves by areas of bondage. For example:

1. I am an alcoholic.
2. I am a drug addict.
3. I am a sex addict.
4. I am a prostitute.
5. I am depressed.
6. I am bipolar.
7. I am schizophrenic.
8. I am obsessive compulsive.
9. I am an angry person.
10. I am not acceptable or worthy.
11. I am not good enough.
12. I am a victim.
13. I am dependent.
14. I am codependent.
15. I am hopeless.

To be defined by a bondage is to say, "I am no longer my own. I am not me. I am what owns me. It is not my fault."

It is destructive when a person stops being troubled by a temptation and starts to be defined by an addiction.

Pick an area of bondage that you deal with. Now see if you can go back and rebuild the lie that has been planted and now has the ability to control your life.

Rebuild it by answering the following questions.

1. **What was the WORD curse or deception that was planted?**
2. **What thoughts accompanied the original word curse that caused it to develop into an IDEA?**
3. **How did that IDEA grow into a BELIEF that was strong enough to control your life?**
4. **What reinforced the curse that caused you to accept the deception as truth?**
5. **How has this IDEA affected your behavior, choices, and actions?**

The Exodus story reveals the condition that develops when a controlling power or bondage is allowed in a life. Under bondage, life gets harder and harder.

Read Exodus 5:6–9

As I read the story of Exodus, I see us battling many of the same issues today. For example, Israel (representing us) was fully under the control of evil as they considered themselves slaves. The Israelites had completely lost the vision of being God's privileged people, designed by Him to be a blessing to the entire human race. Born-again followers of Jesus Christ and His Church can also get caught up in the issues of our contemporary world. When we do, we can drift away from living as representatives of the Lord's Kingdom and start viewing ourselves as slaves to government and the power it possesses.

As any power other than God's power gains a growing advantage over others, the labor associated with bondage gets harder. The Egyptian slave drivers demanded more and more work without mercy. What slavery now demands is all-consuming as it takes over to the point that a way of escape seems impossible. The slave at this point has lost the ability to look for a savior.

In Dylan Klebold's story, bondage was defined as an "entity" that took over his life. The "entity" was allowed because of a word curse planted in his childhood that said, "You are unworthy of love." That WORD planted became an IDEA of revenge. That IDEA became a BELIEF, which resulted in an ACTION of murder and then suicide.

Let's Talk or Think About It

As you read Matthew 17:14–21 consider the following questions.

- **What were the symptoms of the son?**

- **Why do you think the disciples could not heal him?**

- **How did Jesus deal with the sickness of the son?**

- **Do you think some of the sickness we face in America is a result of demonic activity or of a demonic deception that has been planted and has grown into full bondage?**

- **If we take Jesus' answer about having mountain-moving faith, what are we able to do as Ambassadors of God's Kingdom?**

- **What did Jesus say was the limitation for His followers?**

- **If we truly believe Matthew 17:21, how will this change the way we deal with demonic lies, ideas, beliefs, and actions that are causing bondage in people's lives?**

CHAPTER 4

"When Bondage Is Complete"

Hopelessness is arguably the worst condition a person can experience. And it is this hopelessness that gains full control and offers no escape when someone is fully controlled by bondage.

Stories of Tragedy

Early one March morning, Heidi Chamberlain, 15, and her boyfriend Christopher Mills, 16, decided life wasn't worth living. In a story recorded in the Los Angeles Times in March 1996, this young dating couple took a final walk together down a difficult path to a cliff that overlooked the Pacific Ocean near their home. At the location was chain-link fence erected to keep people from the danger of the cliff. Somehow a hole was made in this fence where Heidi and Christopher went through to find themselves at the top of a narrow, concrete spillway. Many of the Los Angeles locals had nicknamed the area "the diving board." Just before dawn on this tragic morning, Heidi and Christopher held hands and jumped off of the 150 foot high cliff landing in the surf of the Pacific below. Just as the sun began to rise, a local jogger found their bodies on the beach. Both of these teenagers left suicide notes stating that they had planned their suicide.

Three months later at San Pedro, a few miles away from Heidi and Christopher's death, two young teenage girls 14-year-old Amber Hernandez and her 15-year-old friend Alicia Hayes came to the decision that life was too hard and hopeless. Again the Los Angeles Times on June 1st of 1996 gave a record of the horrible end of two promising lives. Amber and Alicia went to the cliffs that edged up to the ocean. They methodically tied their hands together making sure that what they were about to do would not be done alone. Their families knew that the girls had been using drugs, but they thought the girls were doing better. The article quoted one of their classmates as they gathered at the cliff to mourn their loss, "You know, life sucks so much as it is now. A lot of teenagers don't know if it's going to get better or not. I guess [suicide] is their only way out. They feel they can't talk to people. We don't feel like we can talk to our parents or anybody. They say they understand. They don't!"

The true stories of Heidi, Christopher, Amber, and Alicia represent a hopelessness that's flooding today's culture in unprecedented ways. To some, life seems so worthless that they are willing not only to kill themselves, but to senselessly murder others as well. Families and communities are left devastated. For others, depression isn't strong enough to make them consider suicide, but it is enough to make them feel lonely, unloved, and miserable.

Many times, this point of hopelessness can bring false solutions such as drugs, alcohol, and other addictions. For many, it brings the ultimate false solution of suicide. The Scriptures tell us that death is exactly what Satan wants for every person on the planet, and he is very good at destroying people caught in his cruel lies. John 10:10 says that, "Satan comes to steal, kill, and destroy."

As we continue to look back at the slavery of the Israelites under the bondage of Egypt, we will see that death has always been the end result of bondage. In Exodus 1:14–16, we can see that Godly offspring are a threat to the power and rule of Satan, so much so that the death of children brings him great delight.

> "So they organized them into work-gangs and put them to hard labor under gang-foremen. They built the storage cities Pithom and Rameses for Pharaoh. But the harder

the Egyptians worked them the more children the Israelites had—children everywhere! The Egyptians got so they couldn't stand the Israelites and treated them worse than ever, crushing them with slave labor. They made them miserable with hard labor—making bricks and mortar and backbreaking work in the fields. They piled on the work, crushing them under the cruel workload.

The king of Egypt had a talk with the two Hebrew midwives; one was named Shiphrah and the other Puah. He said, "When you deliver the Hebrew women, look at the sex of the baby. If it's a boy, kill him; if it's a girl, let her live." (The Message)

Let me review a spiritual foundational truth here about bondage:

1. The word curse (demonic deception) is implanted.
2. The word curse leads to ideas that grow around the curse.
3. The ideas develop into belief where we begin to identify with the lie.
4. Belief guides actions as we start making decisions based on the lie.

From these simple statements, we can draw the following conclusion:

Satan's work is all based on a lie that is controlled by the spirit of fear.

Fear is the main motivational tool of the demonic. As Satan mixes lies with the power of fear, he gains influence over lives, which he continually manipulates toward bondage and the ultimate goal of death.

The first step toward believing Satan's lie is to *doubt* God.

God wanted us to be aware of this scheme when He told us the story of the first man and woman. We know them as Adam and Eve, and the story takes place in Genesis 2 and 3. The following is the core of this demonic scheme designed to get man to doubt God.

Read Genesis 2:15–17

What were God's instructions and intentions for mankind?

Now enters the demonic scheme.

Read Genesis 3:1. Notice that doubting God is suggested. What tools did Satan use to tempt Eve and Adam to sin?

Read Genesis 3:1–5. The demonic deception is now planted.

The basic deception of Satan to every man is that it is better to be god of yourself than it is to trust in the one true God, the Creator of all.

The Downward Spiral

When deception is planted in a life, a progression occurs. This progression is recorded in the first chapter of Romans where it shows the steps that lead to a reprobate mind in those who have rejected Jesus.

> *"For the wrath of God is revealed from heaven against all ungodliness and unrighteousness of men who suppress the truth [a]in unrighteousness, because that which is known about God is evident [b]within them; for God made it evident to them. For since the creation of the world His invisible attributes, His eternal power and divine nature, have been clearly seen, being understood through what has been made, so that they are without excuse. For even though they knew God, they did not honor Him as God or give thanks, but they became futile in their speculations, and their foolish heart was darkened. Professing to be wise, they became fools, and*

exchanged the glory of the incorruptible God for an image in the form of corruptible man and of birds and four-footed animals and crawling creatures.

Therefore, God gave them over in the lusts of their hearts to impurity, so that their bodies would be dishonored among them. For they exchanged the truth of God for a lie, and worshiped and served the creature rather than the Creator, who is blessed forever. Amen.

For this reason God gave them over to degrading passions; for their women exchanged the natural function for that which is unnatural, and in the same way also the men abandoned the natural function of the woman and burned in their desire toward one another, men with men committing [h]indecent acts and receiving in their own persons the due penalty of their error.

*And just as they did not see fit to acknowledge God any longer, God gave them over to a depraved mind, to do those things which are not proper." (*Romans 1:18-28 *NAS)*

When this deception is planted in a life, there is a predictable progression downward.

7 Steps that lead to a Reprobate mind.

1. **Creation Demands a Creator but Man Denies This Truth**

   In verses 18–20, Paul reveals that truth is suppressed by the wicked nature of mankind. He states that the initial step away from godliness is to deny that the first words of Scripture are true: *"In the beginning God created the heavens and the earth."* The wicked nature of mankind believes that creation is a process of natural occurrence based on the theories of evolution and astrophysics. Paul goes on to state that when mankind makes these theories their faith position, they are denying basic facts that are clearly observable.

2. Doubting God

Doubting God, as found in verses 21 and 22, is the basic concept used by Satan to get people moving toward the downward steps of failure. In Genesis 3, we find the story of the serpent tempting Eve to eat of the fruit of the forbidden tree. If you read closely, you will notice that the line Satan uses to get Eve to take a step toward sin involved doubting God.

> *Now the Serpent was more crafty that any of the wild animals the Lord God had made. He said to the woman, "Did God really say, 'You must not eat from any tree in the garden?'"* (Gen.3 NIV)

Doubting God takes all your attention and places it on the problem or the temptation. It is in this condition that belief in God gets hidden and power is given to the test or the temptation. Paul's final words about this stage are that with doubt comes a darkening of the heart. This darkening deceives us into thinking that we are wise when in actuality we have become fools.

Did this open your eyes to areas where Satan has successfully gotten you to doubt God?

List and discuss some possible areas that are controlled by this demonic deception of doubting God.

3. Idolatry and god of Self

When we doubt God, foolishness has become firmly planted in our hearts, and our concept of God turns upside down. Instead of worshipping the Creator God, mankind begins to put attention on material possessions. At this point, humanity forgets God and begins to worship creation. Paul said it like this: "They... exchanged the glory of the immortal God for images made to look like a mortal human being and birds and animals and reptiles."

If Satan is successful in getting us to doubt God, he then tempts us to become god of our own lives.

What are some areas in your life where you attempt control and in essence push God out?

4. **Controlled by Fleshly Desires**

   When God is denied the rightful place within the life of His creation and His creation turns to the worship of things made by man, then the basic desires of the flesh have no guidelines or restraint. Since the drive to reproduce was designed into mankind by God, He gives the directions for its use. So when the first three steps away from God occur, then the next is unrestrained sexual activity. The 1960s in America brought the sexual revolution. Paul says it is the sign that "God gave them over in the sinful desires of their hearts to sexual impurity for the degrading of their bodies with one another."

5. **The Deception Is Fully Accepted**

   In the fifth step of the downward journey, the mind of a person is fully under the control of Satan's lie. We need to remember here that Satan's power is fear. It is through fear that he uses lies and deceptions.

   > *He was a murderer from the beginning, not holding to the truth, for there is not truth in him. When he lies, he speaks his native language, for he is a liar and the father of lies.* (John 8:44 NIV)

   When a person is at this level, Paul says, *"They exchanged the truth about God for a lie, and worshiped and served created things rather than the Creator, who is forever praised."*

6. **Sensuality Turns to Perversion**

   When the human mind is fully under the deception of the demonic, when the human sex drive is no longer restrained and guided by its God-given design, then the next step of darkness enters. In this level of deception, the sex drive is given full reign and full control of the life, so much so that even the basic design for reproduction now becomes inverted and perverted. In this condition, any type of temptation is given freedom to be fulfilled and homosexuality may be fully explored.

> *Because of this, God gave them over to shameful lusts. Even their women exchanged natural sexual relations for unnatural ones. In the same way the men also abandoned natural relations with women and were inflamed with lust for one another. Men committed shameful acts with other men, and received in themselves the due penalty for their error.*

7. **Mind Fully in Bondage**

Some have called this level the "passive wrath of God" because instead of sending judgment for our continued rebellion against His will, He allows us to become god of our own mind. In other words, He allows us to make the same choice that Eve made in the Garden of Eden when she first was deceived by the serpent. The choice of becoming our own god is what Paul called "a depraved mind." In the Greek language, "depraved" is the word adokeemos, which means, "not standing the test, not approved, unfit and spurious." The Webster's Dictionary definition includes the words "foreordain to damnation." Paul describes the contents of a depraved life.

> *They are filled with every kind of unrighteousness, wickedness, covetousness, malice. They are rife with envy, murder, strife, deceit, hostility. They are gossips, 30 slanderers, haters of God, insolent, arrogant, boastful, contrivers of all sorts of evil, disobedient to parents, 31 senseless, covenant-breakers, heartless, ruthless. 32 Although they fully know God's righteous decree that those who practice such things deserve to die, they not only do them but also approve of those who practice them.* (Romans 1:29-32 NET)

We have now come to the very bottom, to the lowest and most broken condition of mankind. We are a slave to the deception of Satan and controlled by the spirit of fear. Such is the condition of mankind apart from the redemptive work of God.

Let's Talk or Think About It

- **Based on the areas as described in Romans chapter 1, at what level of bondage do you find yourself (or others)?**

- **If a person has become aware of their personal sin condition and has gone by faith to ask Jesus to forgive them and to receive Him into their life, do you think that the process of reprobation can still be harming a person?**

We have now thoroughly looked at bondage. We have looked at aspects such as what it is, how it starts, how it develops, the demonic deception, and its progression. We have even looked at our personal areas of bondage.

Now it is time to start finding our *way out*! Chapter 5 begins the next important step of our journey. This section is called, "THE TURNING POINT."

SECTION #2
The Turning Point

CHAPTER 5

"When The Worst Becomes The Best"

After being in the pastoral ministry for nearly 40 years, I have walked with many people through some very difficult times, and a pattern has emerged. Sometimes the worst points in a person's life become the very places where they have found the unlimited presence and provision of God.

Oddly enough, one of these worst-of-times-best-of-times events happened to me after I had been in church work for over 35 years. Through all of the years of being raised in a pastor's home, attending college to get an education in music so that I could work in a church worship ministry, attending Seminary to prepare for ministry, attending all of the latest and greatest seminars on how to have a successful church, doing student ministry work for fourteen years, and eventually becoming a church planter for 26 years, I finally *hit the wall*. I came to the *end of my rope*. My car ran *out of road*. I came to a _turning point_. Or whatever else you say when you have finally come to the lowest and most painful place in your life. I could no longer continue in the direction I was going in the condition I was in.

An old country comedian named Jerry Clower used to tell the story of a time he was raccoon hunting and his dogs chased a raccoon up a tree. His job that night was to climb the tree to capture the raccoon. He had spent most of the night fighting with that raccoon, and at about daylight, one of his friends showed up and Jerry called down to him and said, "Shoot up in this tree. One of us needs some relief." This is the place you end up when continuing without change is simply not an option. We either turn to God or we turn to some kind of final relief.

For me, the pastoral ministry had become a burden too heavy to carry. What started out as a teenager's desire to help people and lead them to redemption and restoration through Jesus had morphed into something very unhealthy. After years of education, conferences, and seminars on how to build the "successful" church, I had taken on the responsibility of personally building something that could be viewed as success. In a well-intentioned way, I had taken on the role of "god" for the church.

When I read the scripture in Matthew 11:30 where Jesus said, "My yoke is easy and My burden is light," I must confess that on the inside I would say, "That is absolutely not true because what I am feeling is not easy and it certainly is not light. As a matter of fact, it is about to crush me." I honestly believed that the effectiveness of the church completely depended on ME and my ability to lead it, train it, and direct it. Most of the pastoral training that I received was about preparing me to do the work of ministry. Somewhere in that process, I got my proverbial train completely off track, and the work involved in moving the church "train" required striving, straining, and manipulating everything and everybody to get the work done.

All of this self-effort started crashing down around my shoulders and God started pruning my life.

It all started for me in the fall of 2010 when I felt that the Lord told me that He was about to do a work of pruning in this 10-year-old church plant.

Pruning is a horticultural term in which a gardener uses a sharp cutting instrument to remove unnecessary branches from a fruit tree. The purpose of pruning is to remove any competing limbs so that the fruit-bearing branches can receive more of the life found in the trunk of the tree, thus producing better and stronger fruit. He led me to personally study this concept and then to instruct the church on John 15:1–17 so that we would be prepared for a season of pruning at the hands of the "vine dresser."

Read John 15:1–17

This is what I discovered from this passage.

1. Jesus is the True Vine where life is found
2. Father God is the one who does the work of pruning.
3. The purpose of pruning is twofold. One purpose is to remove branches that do not bear fruit. The second purpose is to prune back branches that do bear fruit so that they can bear more fruit.
4. The message of Jesus is to call His own to remain in Him. Remaining in Him allows us to be fruitful. If we do not remain, it is impossible for us to be effective.
5. There is a very powerful promise given to those who remain. Verse 7 says, "If you remain in Me and my words remain in you, ask whatever you wish, and it will be given you."

Although there are many great truths in this passage, I discovered very quickly that I did not fully know what this message meant. But, I was soon to find out as God began His pruning.

The **first area of pruning** involved removing and readjusting some of the main leaders of our church family. Three large cuts were made within a two-month period. One was an elder that resigned and left the church after the Pastor/Elder team had a conversation encouraging each other to be examples of people living by faith in the Lord and in the disciplines of scripture.

The **second area of pruning** came as one of the founding pastors of the church was asked to pursue the clear calling of God on His life. His calling was to develop a mission-training center that would train people to go to the unreached people groups of the world.

The **third area of pruning** came as there were several families of the church that took offense at the elder resignation and the calling of one of the founding pastors to his next ministry placement. Because of this offense, 13 families left the church. They left with hurt feelings and resentment.

The **fourth area of pruning** came as the student pastor received a calling to another ministry and left within a few weeks of the previous cuts. This resulted in the loss of even more families from the church.

The **fifth area of pruning** came in me. I felt so many negative feelings at this time that I became completely numb. The two main emotions I felt were hurt and terror. I felt like a personal failure because I thought it was my job to run the church, to protect the work of the Lord, and to lead the church in becoming a success. This false belief had so engulfed my mind that I was completely unaware that I was living in bondage. All I could see at the time was that I was a complete personal failure. I felt I had **failed** myself, my family, and my God!

On top of that, many of the families that left the church, left with the intention to protest the pruning and to cause the church and the remaining leaders to hurt and fail. I felt deep levels of betrayal because of that. Rejection is one of the most painful feelings a person can experience. And adding the pain of that rejection on top of the feelings of personal failure, the word "hurt" did not begin to describe the level of pain I felt for almost 12 months.

This was the worst period of time that I had ever experienced and even more than what I thought could be possible. However, it was in this part of my journey that I call, "The Valley of the Shadow of Death," that I found my TURNING POINT.

Have you experienced a TURNING POINT in your life? Take time to retell that story. (If you are in a small group, let a few share their turning point story.)

It was in the depths of this despair that the Lord began to speak to me LIFE CHANGING WORDS.

His *first word* to me was:

Take your hands off of My Church, and I will build My Church and the gates of Hades will not overcome it. (see Matthew 16:18 NIV)

I had not realized it, but I had believed the deception that I was responsible for His church. With this belief firmly in place, there came the rush of pride if the church succeeded in the eyes of men and the crush of failure if it did not impress others. I was somehow blinded by the deception that it was my job to build His Church, and I had given almost all of my adult life to accomplish this goal. I must tell you that this deception that I bought into had been a slave master in my life and had kept me in bondage for a very long time. The truth is, when God builds His church, it will be so powerful that even death, the grave, and hell will not be able to stand against it.

His *second word* to me was:

Seek first the Kingdom of God and His righteousness, and all these things will be given to you as well. (Matthew 6:33 NIV)

My commission was to know God, learn to hear His voice, and operate in obedience to the revelation of His Word. My ministry was to release the will of the Lord's Kingdom into every life and situation in which I would come in contact. My prayer was to be patterned after the model prayer in Matthew 6 when Jesus prayed, "Your Kingdom come, Your will be done on earth as it is in heaven."

His *third word* to me was:

I AM sovereign God and I am in charge of all things.

There was great relief for me in this message because I now realized that God is in charge and responsible for His church and I am not. He is so in control that we have this confidence: *"And we know that in all things God works for the good of those who love Him, who have been called according to His purpose."* (Romans 8:28)

In this revelation, I was able to resign from the position of god of myself and the ownership of the church. This was a tremendous relief, and for the first time I did not feel the crushing weight of the ministry. I did not even realize that this had developed in my life. But, coming to this turning point in my life, I had to fully admit that I was not God and that all of my efforts had turned into a horrible mess. By realizing He is sovereign God in charge of all things, I handed my life and my mess back over to Him.

His *fourth word* to me was:

> *I am going to fulfill Psalm 23 in your life.*

He fulfilled all of His promises in this Great Shepherd passage for me following the season of pruning. He literally gave me a season of lying down in green pastures. He let me experience quiet waters instead of the raging storm that happened earlier. He restored my soul. Now I am more sensitive to Him leading me in paths of righteousness. Even in my "valley of death" experiences, I have found that I do not have to fear things because His presence is powerful and strong there. I can now live fully in His Spirit and bounty even though enemies remain. He anoints me with oil of the Holy Spirit for effective ministry and anointing, and my confidence is now in the Lord and not in my efforts.

I wanted to share my most recent "turning point" experience with you so you might see in my failure that God is at work in all of our lives to fulfill His promise in the book of Romans:

> *"Because those whom he foreknew he also predestined* **to be conformed to the image of his Son**, *that his Son would be the firstborn among many brothers and sisters. And those he predestined, he also called; and those he called, he also justified; and those he justified, he also glorified. What then shall we say about these things? If God is for us, who can be against us?"* (Romans 8:29-31 NET)

This is my story of how the <u>worst</u> becomes the <u>best</u>. It was a spiritual turning point. But, let me share one more example of how God works through suffering.

At the same time the Lord was doing a great work in me personally, something else happened in one of our worship services. A young family in our church who had their world "rocked" when their first child was born with VATER syndrome experienced something from God that brought supernatural healing into their family and at the same time set the church on spiritual fire. This event happened about one year after we went through the pruning I shared in the previous story.

When Amari was born she had a condition called VATER Syndrome. It is a condition that involves several problems, but the main issue was that her esophagus didn't connect to her stomach and instead ended in a connection to her lung. Within a month of her birth, the doctors realized that Amari would never be able to eat food because the food consumed would simply be lodged in her lung and cause perpetual pneumonia. The only option left was to place a feeding port in her stomach where a specially prepared nutrient mixture would be placed three times a day to keep her alive. The family saw several doctors and specialists who all told the family that if they didn't find the problem and fix it quickly, Amari wouldn't live to see her twenties.

Let me allow you to read the rest of the story as told to me by her mother, Chelsea.

> *We spoke with her surgeon and he informed us that the only other option was to do a very invasive surgery where they go in through her side, cutting her ribs in order to locate the connection and remove it permanently. This was the last thing we wanted for Amari. She had been through so much in her short 5 ½ years and an open chest surgery was not sounding like an easy thing for her to endure.*
>
> *The Sunday before we were supposed to leave for St. Louis, our church brought our family before the congregation, and*

they had the entire children's ministry gather around Amari and all of the adults gather around my husband and me. These kids poured out their hearts and began praying and asking God for healing for Amari. It was an amazing sight to see all of these children with the same faith that Amari has shown, crying out to God.

That Sunday after church, a woman came to me and shared that God had revealed to her that Amari had been healed. That was a lot for us as parents to swallow, but we had seen him do it before and believed that he could do it again. After church, we went out to eat for lunch and I noticed that Amari was stealing bites of baked potato from my plate and not even coughing. She took some drinks of my sweet tea and still nothing happened. We went for dessert and Amari was eating frozen yogurt without any trouble at all. We started to realize that there had been a change and Amari was able to eat and drink without trouble for the first time in her life. The next day we still made the trip up to St. Louis to meet the doctors. They did several tests that were supposed to lead up to her open chest surgery. Every test throughout the week came back confirming what we already knew........Amari had been HEALED!

By the end of the week, they wanted to do one final test to see if they could find anything. When the doctor came out of the room after her test, he told us that they had found that there was no longer a connection between her esophagus and trachea, and her lungs look great and were in the best shape that they had ever seen them. PRAISE GOD!!!!!! They let us leave the hospital that same day and we were so happy that there was no need for surgery!

The turning point for Amari, for Amari's family, and for our church family came as God brought with Him a creative miracle of healing. This healing happened in front of our church family and turned the previous season of pruning into a season of faith-filled revival that began the restoration of the church.

Why do you think the story of Amari was a turning point in the church?

Do you think God provides a turning point for everyone?

Israel's turning point came as Moses began to obey the Lord.

> *Moses returned to the Lord, and said, "Lord, why have you caused trouble for this people? Why did you ever send me? From the time I went to speak to Pharaoh in your name, he has caused trouble for this people, and you have certainly not rescued them!" Then the Lord said to Moses, "Now you will see what I will do to Pharaoh, for compelled by my strong hand he will release them, and by my strong hand he will drive them out of his land."*
>
> *God spoke to Moses and said to him, "I am the Lord. I appeared to Abraham, to Isaac, and to Jacob as God Almighty, but by my name 'the Lord' I was not known to them. 4 I also established my covenant with them to give them the land of Canaan, where they were living as resident foreigners. I have also heard the groaning of the Israelites, whom the Egyptians are enslaving, and I have remembered my covenant. Therefore, tell the Israelites, 'I am the Lord. I will bring you out from your enslavement to the Egyptians, I will rescue you from the hard labor they impose, and I will redeem you with an outstretched arm and with great judgments. I will take you to myself for a people, and I will be your God. Then you will know that I am the Lord your God, who brought you out from your enslavement to the Egyptians. I will bring you to the land I swore to give to*

Abraham, to Isaac, and to Jacob—and I will give it to you as a possession. I am the Lord!'" (Exodus 5:22-6:8 NET)

- I will bring you out from under the yoke (bondage) of the Egyptians (representing evil). (Ex. 6:6)

- I will free you from being slaves to them. (Ex. 6:6)

- I will redeem you with an outstretched arm and with mighty acts of judgment. (Ex. 6:6)

- I will take you as My own people and I will be your God. (Ex. 6:7)

- I will bring you to the land of promise that I swore with uplifted hand to give to Abraham, to Isaac, and to Jacob. I will give it to you as a possession. (Ex. 6:8)

There are times when our personal sin and slavery to the enemy take us to the bottom of our existence.

When the emotional pain along with spiritual death in our lives begins to open the door for hopelessness, there is an inner pain that gives us only two options.

The first is to find a way to remove the pain on our own. This comes in many forms such as drugs, alcohol, and escape through any means necessary. Some even take their own life.

But there is a second option: We find ourselves lying on our backs at the bottom of our pit and we cry out to God. We confess our sins or weaknesses and our failures. We give up trying to be god of our own lives, and from a desperate spirit, we call out for God to forgive our sins and fill us with His life. We finally allow Him to become the master of our lives. At this point, we begin to hear His words of life. He begins to speak to us and lead us. He begins to show us His plan for our lives. He lifts us off of the bottom and supplies a new hope. It is a TURNING POINT that is so appreciated that once you receive it, you will forever be grateful.

For I consider that the sufferings of this present time are not worthy to be compared with the glory that is to be revealed to us. For the anxious longing of the creation waits eagerly for the revealing of the sons of God. For the creation was subjected to futility, not willingly, but because of Him who subjected it, in hope 21 that the creation itself also will be set free from its slavery to corruption into the freedom of the glory of the children of God. (Romans 8:18-21 NAS)

Let's Talk or Think About It

- What life-changing message(s) did your receive from God when you were lying flat on your back at the bottom of your pit?

- Take time to re-read Exodus 5:22-6:8 and list or share with your small group what God shows you when you get to a TURING POINT.

- Why do you think God allows us to get to this "end of the rope" experience in our life?

- What is it about humanity that requires this awful TURNING POINT experience before we get our life right with our Creator? (Use Ephesians 2 as a guideline)

CHAPTER 6

"Where A Redeemer Is Found"

A life crisis usually comes at the natural end of a bondage progression. Many times our search for real answers about life comes only after all of our efforts at managing or being god of our own lives fail. Now don't get me wrong; I don't think any of us say to ourselves, "I want to be god of my life." But, that is exactly what we end up doing as we try to design and run every facet of our lives. Because of our humanity, we have a very limited ability to control our own destiny. Humanity comes with great inadequacies. So naturally when this journey of self-management hits a wall of failure and pain, it gives us a great opportunity to say, "Ok, what I have been doing is not working, so let me look at other options."

The reality is that we all must come to the end of ourselves in order to start looking for a better, stronger, and clearer way to live. This is when our real life search begins.

What are some things you have trusted in that have let you down?

A Different Kind of Guy

Kyle showed up one day at a newly forming church that was meeting temporarily in a circus tent as a new worship center was being constructed. Kyle was in his mid-forties. He was a child of the 60s, fully bought into the hippie movement as shown by his waist-length hair, bell-bottom jeans, and silky shirt with baggy sleeves along with the required headband. The challenge for Kyle was twofold. Not only was he attending church for the first time in 30 years, but also he was still inebriated from the previous night's activities, a habit built upon a lifetime of looking for chemicals to help him cope with his hopelessness.

He came to church that day because a new friend had invited him to attend and to share in the free lunch that was going to be provided after service. Kyle was a huge fan of the band, "Lynyrd Skynyrd," so he liked his music loud and rocky with a southern twist. Fortunately, Kyle stumbled (literally) into a church that used a band with enough rock style to pique his interest.

So began the development of a friendship between a 60s rocker with a newly forming church that valued people. This form of acceptance was just what Kyle needed. Some churches have developed their own form of legalism that would have subtly or overtly pushed someone like Kyle out the back door. But, because this group of believers fully accepted that we are all broken by sin and the sinfulness of our world, they simply reached out and loved this "different" kind of guy.

Kyle started developing a friendship with the pastor of this new church by calling him once a week at approximately 2:30 in the morning. Every time Kyle called to talk, he was either high on some drug or drunk. His introduction on the phone was, "Is this that rock and roll preacher?" Somehow, in God's divine comedic plan, this 60s rocker fell in love with the people of the church and the church fell in love with him. After about six months of this unusual partnership, Kyle started seeing something in the Christ followers that he liked. He started hearing the message of forgiveness, purpose, and hope, and he became a true seeker attempting to find if there was something authentic in this life through Jesus.

Then one normal Sunday morning, Kyle stepped out of his chair in the audience and walked forward to talk with the pastor. With tears in his eyes, he told the pastor that he wanted to know Jesus. He was tired of the emptiness and hopelessness that he had experienced in his life. He was ready to take that leap of faith, to trust that Jesus would forgive his sin and to let Him take over his life. It was a glorious day when the people of the church celebrated the salvation of their new brother in Christ.

The church was proud that Kyle did not change his hippie style at all. Now he was a 60s rocker who loved Jesus and celebrated the forgiveness he had found.

God Sends a Redeemer

In the ongoing story of Israel, the Jews were in an intensifying bondage to the Pharaoh of Egypt. The slavery was brutal, the work was more difficult than humans were designed to accomplish, and hopelessness was causing their lives to become darker and harder. God our Creator saw the condition of His chosen people and He desired to send a leader who would help lead them out of slavery and into a land of freedom and blessing. God spoke to Moses, who was an adopted son of the Pharaoh.

Read Exodus 3:1–10

Who was Moses before God spoke to him?

Is there a time you have had a burning bush type of experience when God spoke to you?

There are some important points from this story to consider:

- God sees the damage done by bondage. He desires that those in bondage be given an opportunity to find freedom. God cares for broken and enslaved people.

- God makes it clear that a redeemer is needed to lead people out of bondage.

- God sends a redeemer to everyone in bondage. All they must do is to follow by faith the Lord's plan out of their misery.

- For Israel, the redeemer was Moses.

- For Kyle, the Redeemer was Jesus and His representatives in a local church.

Although God sent a redeemer through Moses, the Israelites messed up their journey out of bondage in many ways. They were tempted to bring in the worship of false gods and idols. They were tempted to practice the ways of the idolatrous people they lived around. They misjudged God's plan for redemption and false redeemers tempted them. Many in Israel never got to experience the freedom and blessing of God.

In the 1960s, America messed up as she attempted to find new freedoms from sin and be politically correct, which hid God and especially His Son, Jesus, as redeemer from our society. Because of this trend, people in bondage have begun to call just about anything a "higher power."

Not everyone and not every belief is the Redeemer sent by God. There are many people and religions that promise hope or freedom, but the true Redeemer of our day is the One and Only Son of God. He is Jesus of Nazareth, the long-awaited Messiah. Any other search after a "higher power" will lead only to a false hope that never reaches freedom.

Let's Talk or Think About It

- **What are some current "higher powers" offered by this world?**

- **What happens when we put our faith and trust in false promises, false gods, or idols?**

- **Moses was an Old Testament redeemer. How was he like the redeemer of the New Testament, which is Jesus Christ?**

- **What are you trusting in as the redeemer for your life and why?**

CHAPTER 7

"Where A Leap Of Faith Is Required"

Heights scare me to death; so working from an extension ladder is pure agony for me. To watch people who work on skyscrapers, cell towers, or anything else over 3 feet above the ground is something I just cannot understand. Most of us tend to dread those events or activities that make us feel out of control. Perhaps it is the thought of a significant life change that scares you. Possibly it is a situation that does not follow your plan, and you begin to feel out of control.

We have come to the point in our journey from bondage where we are nearing the edge of a cliff. This is the point where a decision is required. There are two options: One, you can turn around and go back into your bondage, because the fear of the next step forward makes the slave life look appealing at this moment. Or two, you make the decision to run toward freedom and commit to taking a "leap of faith." This is where the decision to give our life over to a redeemer stands right in front of us.

In reality, whenever we take the step of faith into the promise of a redeemer, it can cause great fear. What if the redeemer is not real or our faith ends in some kind of disaster?

Let's take a moment and look at some of the "false redeemers" who offer some kind of fake answers to our bondage, but in reality have <u>no power</u> to rescue.

Material Possessions / Economic Security

We all want to feel secure financially, but the reality of an economic crisis, a healthcare bill, a job loss, or a hundred other things can come along and remove this security. Plus, somewhere deep down we know that the best financial security can do for us, is to keep us "comfortable" while alive on this earth. What about after death?

Another Person To Complete You

Every Hallmark or Lifetime movie on television paints the picture that the only thing you need for security, fulfillment, and real life is to fall in love. A great marriage and 2.5 kids will cause us all to live happily ever after. A little reality shows us that relationships can be a blessing, but they also always end. This leaves us asking, "Where is security found that carries over even after death?"

Government

As socialism increases in America, there is a growing dependence on government. This utopian ideal inevitably fails as the government takes more and more from the working class to provide for the dependent class. As soon as the working class runs out of money there comes the easily foreseeable collapse. Not only does government fail to provide a secure survival on this planet, but it also does nothing to address what happens to us after this life is over.

Position Or Status

So much effort of our life is put into achieving position or status in our society. This energy output is given in an effort to define the purpose of our existence. We seem to be driven to believe that life's meaning comes from having others see us as important or successful. There is a real fallacy associated with this particular search. Within human relationships there are no true securities. For one day, you may find yourself a HERO, but on the next day you may find yourself a HEEL to the same eyes. The reality of this search is that it fills our days with busyness, but does nothing to answer the deeper questions about the purpose of life.

Islam

Islam is a religion that is basically the direct opposite of and in conflict with Judaism and Christianity. In this religion, the main purpose in life is to advance Islam around the world with Sharia law guiding the society. To live a life acceptable to their prophet Mohammad or to guarantee eternal security requires becoming a martyr for this cause. This would include killing others who do not agree or convert to Islam.

Buddhism

Buddhism follows the wisdom and sayings of Buddha. It promotes advancement toward Nirvana, where the normal attachments of this world and this body are overcome. They must adhere to a strict set of rules. This religion also incorporates all other religions, meaning the belief that there are many ways to God. There is no real security in this life. Buddhism suggests only the hope of an afterlife, but no sure way to find it.

Hinduism

Hinduism is based on the concept of reincarnation. This faith believes that the life you currently live is based upon the quality of the life you lived in a previous cycle. The motive of the faith is to improve the station of your next life. There is no redeemer here, only a legalistic system that pushes a person toward a purer life with the false hope of another life.

Agnosticism

This religion advocates that there may be a creator God, but He is so advanced and aloof from us that there is no way to know him at all. There is no security in this life and no hope for a life after death.

Atheism

I've always said that this belief system requires the biggest act of faith. To put your faith in the premise that there is no God is a very large act of faith. To believe there is no God means all that remains is survival of the fittest on this earth because there is no hope for life after death.

Drugs Or Alcohol

There are many others who look much lower for some type of answer to the deep and burning questions of life. For some, the questions are too deep to fathom and the pains of our sinful nature too powerful to fight. The next best solution for those in this condition seems to focus on finding a way to numb the pain. Although this form of self-medication may offer moments of pain reduction, it never changes the reality of our condition. And to make things worse, this path leads many to the ravages of addiction without answers to their deep questions.

Sex Without Relationship

In America, in the 1960's, a sexual revolution promised that fulfilling the human sex drive without moral guidelines or Christian principles was the new way to find freedom and purpose in life. But, this experiment left people feeling used and lonely and has paved the way for a massive number of abortions, sexually transmitted diseases, and sexual perversions. One of the great catastrophes of this social experiment is the weakening of the family. This weakening is truly leading to the failure of the American culture.

The search for false gods can go on and on. It is quite normal for humanity to search through what the world offers to see if a redeemer can be found. In my personal search, each of these false gods offered no hope for my broken condition, no satisfying answers about life, and no real hope for life after death. I found them to be false gods with false promises that would end in hopelessness. I could never leap in their direction.

As you began to understand that being god of your own life was not working, what were some of the ways (other than Jesus) you looked at which seemed to promise meaning, purpose, and hope for this life and the life to come?

What were the results of your search after you pursued the false promises of those things listed above?

Let me attempt to share with you the God who created us, who loves us, who paid for our brokenness, and who gives us hope in this life and in the life to come.

The picture of salvation and redemption is first introduced to the Israeli slaves just before Pharaoh (a representative of Satan) released them. This fascinating story is written in Exodus and it is called the Passover.

> *While the Israelites were still in the land of Egypt, the Lord gave the following instructions to Moses and Aaron: "From now on, this month will be the first month of the year for you. Announce to the whole community of Israel that on the tenth day of this month each family must choose a lamb or a young goat for a sacrifice, one animal for each household. If a family is too small to eat a whole animal, let them share with another family in the neighborhood. Divide the animal according to the size of each family and how much they can eat. The animal you select must be a one-year-old male, either a sheep or a goat, with no defects.*
>
> *Take special care of this chosen animal until the evening of the fourteenth day of this first month. Then the whole assembly of the community of Israel must slaughter their lamb or young goat at twilight. They are to take some of the blood and smear it on the sides and top of the door frames of the houses where*

they eat the animal. That same night they must roast the meat over a fire and eat it along with bitter salad greens and bread made without yeast. Do not eat any of the meat raw or boiled in water. The whole animal—including the head, legs, and internal organs—must be roasted over a fire. Do not leave any of it until the next morning. Burn whatever is not eaten before morning.

These are your instructions for eating this meal: Be fully dressed, wear your sandals, and carry your walking stick in your hand. Eat the meal with urgency, for this is the Lord's Passover. On that night I will pass through the land of Egypt and strike down every firstborn son and firstborn male animal in the land of Egypt. I will execute judgment against all the gods of Egypt, for I am the Lord! But the blood on your doorposts will serve as a sign, marking the houses where you are staying. When I see the blood, I will pass over you. This plague of death will not touch you when I strike the land of Egypt. (Exodus 12:1-14 NLT)

The foreshadowing we see in the Passover story of salvation through Jesus in the New Testament is a beautiful picture. There are many symbols of this ancient event that match perfectly with what Jesus did for us on the cross. Let me give you just a few of the main points.

1. The Lamb to be sacrificed was a perfect lamb. When John the Baptist saw Jesus coming he said, *"Look, the Lamb of God, who takes away the sin of the world."* (John 1:29 NIV)
2. Sin always ends in judgment, just as God promised judgment on all the gods of Egypt. Sin's result is death. *"The wages of sin is death."* (Romans 6:23 NIV)
3. The blood of the sacrificial lamb was to be painted on the door frame of the house. This was the sign to God that this person or family was protected. Jesus spilt his blood on the Roman cross. It is His blood, when received by faith that covers a sinner's life. Jesus said this about His blood: *"This is my blood of the covenant,*

which is poured out for many for the forgiveness of sins." (Matthew 16:28 NIV)

Jesus the Messiah

Let's look a little closer at Jesus the Messiah. Here are some of the things He said about Himself.

> *Come to Me, all you who labor and are heavy laden, and I will give you rest. 29 Take My yoke upon you and learn from Me, for I am gentle and lowly in heart, and you will find rest for your souls. 30 For My yoke is easy and My burden is light."* (Matthew 11:28-30 NKJV)

When we attempt to be god of our own lives, the weight of that responsibility and the work of that effort is fatiguing. This weariness comes from being under the weight of bondage. Jesus offers a rest for all caught in bondage. To be a believer and a follower of Jesus, you must be willing to take upon your life His teaching. Scripture likened Jesus' teaching to a yoke. The yoke is not the yellow part of an egg, but rather a wooden beam that has been shaped to fit on the neck of an ox. This yoke was then attached to a pull-cart or farm implement. It literally meant a weight or a burden. Then Jesus described His yoke as easy and His burden as light. Here you can find rest by trusting and following Him.

> *Jesus answered, "Most assuredly, I say to you, unless one is born of water and the Spirit, he cannot enter the kingdom of God. 6 That which is born of the flesh is flesh, and that which is born of the Spirit is spirit. 7 Do not marvel that I said to you, 'You must be born again.'* (John 3:5-7 NKJV)

To be made right with God, a person must have their spirit made alive by God's Spirit. Romans 3:23, tells us why being born again is so important: *"For all have sinned and fall short of the glory of God, and are justified freely by His grace through the redemption [redeemer] that came by Christ Jesus."*

Romans 6:23 says, *"For the wages of sin is death, but the gift of God is eternal life in Christ Jesus our Lord."* To attempt to make this clear, let me say that our spirit is dead because of our sin and this sin condition is common to all mankind. If our spirit remains dead, we miss the entire purpose for our life and the opportunity for eternal life in God's Kingdom.

Let's Talk or Think About It

- **How did you discover that Jesus the Messiah, the only Son of God, had come to be your redeemer?**

- **How did God get His message of salvation to you?**

- **The "leap of faith" that we talked about earlier is now before us. Take a few moments to think or talk about what the "leap of faith" was like for you.**

- **What were the fears you had to move past?**

This is the focus and purpose of the Holy Scriptures. So here is where the leap is to begin.

To Be Born Again

To be "born again," a person must simply understand a few basic things.

First, is the realization that I am a sinner and have broken the right and wrong laws of God that are defined in the *Ten Commandments*. Exodus 20 records these commandments:

- You shall have no other gods before Me.
- You shall not make for yourself an idol.
- You shall not misuse the name of the Lord your God.
- Remember the Sabbath day by keeping it holy.
- Honor your father and your mother.

- You shall not murder.
- You shall not commit adultery.
- You shall not steal.
- You shall not give false testimony against your neighbor.
- You shall not covet your neighbor's house, manservant or maidservant, his ox or donkey, or anything that belongs to your neighbor.

My default setting is often to go against the will of God as revealed in the Holy Scriptures. Because of sin, my spirit is dead. It is that part of us that is highlighted when we find ourselves at the end of a busy and distracted day, when the noise of life is turned off and we find ourselves alone in our bed. It is in that moment of quietness that we realize something is wrong within us. We feel empty, incomplete, even broken.

**Jesus, the Messiah, knew our sin condition
that leaves us broken and the judgment that
accompanies it, so He gave himself
as our sin payment when He died on the cross.**

Believing in Jesus and His great payment on the cross is the <u>first step</u> in finding a solution for our sinful condition. Once we have heard the good news that there is a solution to our sin condition, then with faith like a child, we simply confess to Jesus our lost and broken condition.

Next, by faith we receive His forgiveness, which He willingly gives to everyone who believes in His name. Once the faith step in Jesus is taken, the Lord gives forgiveness and we are immediately set free from our sin condition and from the impending judgment that sin brings. In this cleansed and forgiven position, we are now prepared to invite the Spirit of Jesus to come into our hearts to become the new master (God) of our lives. The Apostle Paul says that salvation comes when we confess our sins.

Read Romans 10:9-10

As a guide, let me give you a simple prayer that might help you as you invite Jesus to become the redeemer of your life.

> *Dear Jesus,*
>
> *I come to you today as a sinful and broken person. I believe that you are God's Son and that you died on the cross to pay for my sin condition. I also believe that you are now able to hear my cry for help. My requests are to please forgive me of my sin, cleanse me from the filth and death of sin, come into my spirit and make it alive, and take over my life as my Forgiver and Master. Thank you for forgiving me, for filling me, and for giving me your life. Amen.*

This is how you begin your new relationship with your redeemer. Jesus is the true Redeemer, and when He has forgiven you, made your spirit alive, and taken over the God position of your life, **you are transformed**. With this transformation by our Redeemer, Jesus, we now begin to walk in a brand new type of life.

Israel's first steps out of slavery in Egypt required a lot of faith. Although they longed for freedom, the beginning steps of the journey made them face a lot of fear. Scripture records this part of their journey out of bondage.

Read Exodus 13:17-22

Observations

Here are a few truths revealed about the new journey of your life as you follow your Redeemer (Jesus) out of bondage.

First, God will lead you through a period of freedom in which it is easy to enjoy your new relationship with Jesus. Some call it the "spiritual honeymoon," which is usually for a period of time immediately after you have accepted Jesus. This time period is characterized by celebration of your new life in Christ.

Second, after the honeymoon period there will be some spiritual battles you will have to fight as you move toward your freedom and abundance found in Jesus. At these challenges, you will be tempted to return to your slavery because the intensity of the battle may seem overwhelming. We will deal with winning these battles in a later chapter.

Thirdly, God led Israel by a pillar of cloud by day and a pillar of fire by night. When following Jesus our Redeemer, God also gives us two ways to follow His plan for our lives. He gives us His Word (Scripture) and the Holy Spirit who now dwells within us to lead us into all truth.

Let's Talk or Think About It

- **Read Matthew 7:13–14. Now break this verse apart and see if you can find what Jesus was revealing about salvation and redemption in these verses.**

  The Narrow Gate:

  The Wide Gate:

  The Broad Road that leads to destruction:

  The Narrow Road that leads to life:

- **Why do you think only a few find the narrow gate and road?**

- **What could we do practically that would help people who have entered the Wide Gate and the Broad Road that is leading them toward destruction?**

CHAPTER 8

"Where All Things Become New"

We have now come to a very important part of our journey. We have spent several chapters looking at life stories that reveal what bondage is and how it destroys our lives and dooms us for eternity. Since we found a redeemer in Jesus, we now need a new mental picture of what God has in mind for those who have chosen to follow Him as Savior and Lord.

When Adam and Eve sinned, God's design for humanity became marred and broken. Mankind's original design allowed him to walk with God, talk with God, rule over God's creation, and in general, live a life of blessing and intimacy with God. There was no sin, sickness, or even death in God's original design. But, with the entrance of the serpent, Satan tempted Adam and Eve to doubt God and to take up the role of god of themselves. This is where everything started going wrong and led to Satan causing sin, sickness, rebellion, curse, and abuse to wreck humanity.

Then God sent His Son, Jesus the Messiah, to provide a way for mankind to regain all that was lost in the fall of mankind. In this chapter, we will look at many of the ways that following Jesus will restore us to full redemption.

When God saw Israel in slavery, He came to Moses and told him about the place He had prepared for His people.

Read Exodus 3:7–8

It is vital that we know what God has designed for us now that He is our God and the director of our lives.

One of the biggest challenges for a Christ follower is to know, understand, and believe what God has made him or her to be.

To help you find areas that attempt to keep you in bondage to the "old lost condition," ask yourself this question:

What is the biggest thing in my life that keeps me from living what God has designed for me?

Let's start at the beginning of the Holy Scriptures in the book of Genesis and discover God's intended design and purpose for our lives.

Read Genesis 1:26–30

Based on Genesis 1:26–30, what was God's full intention for man's life?

Observations of Our Original Purpose

We are made in the image of God. One way to grasp this, is found in the three-part nature of man which represents the Trinity of God.

GOD	**MANKIND**
Creator/ Father	Soul (Mind, Will, Emotions)
Jesus Christ	Physical
Holy Spirit	spirit

We were designed to rule over fish, birds, livestock, all wild animals, and all other creatures of the earth. The word "rule over" in the original Hebrew is 'radah,' pronounced raw-dah, and it means to have dominion over or to rule God's creation. It was God's intention that His people who walked with Him in close relationship and were under His rule would have children and populate the earth so that the entire earth would be modeled after the prototype. God then provided man with everything he needed to survive on planet Earth.

Evil Enters Man's Existence

Then something happened that broke the plan of God—God's creation fell under the power of evil.

This was revealed as Scripture records again in Genesis.

Read Genesis 3:1–6

The practical meaning of the narrative of the fall of mankind is that man was tempted by Satan to take the position of god. This was the fruit of the Tree of the Knowledge of Good and Evil. The result was that the spirit part of man died. Mankind then began the struggle of attempting to become good enough to earn God's favor and to regain the life of the spirit they lost.

This is why we are broken. Our spirits are dead in trespass and sin and our attempts at being god of our own lives are like a blind and deaf person attempting to lead someone else. We have no chance!

Evil is a part of our earthly existence because of Lucifer, one of the three amazing creations of God known as archangels. The trio of these magnificent creatures has the names Gabriel, Michael, and Lucifer. The one named Lucifer caused a rebellion in heaven that brought evil into our world.

The Prophet Ezekiel gives us a glimpse of the magnificence of the angel God described as Lucifer.

Read Ezekiel 28:12–15

Then the prophets give us a glimpse of why Lucifer was kicked out of heaven. The reason for Lucifer's fall from heaven is recorded in the prophecies of Isaiah and Ezekiel.

Continue in Ezekiel 28:16–17

Because of this prideful rebellion, this magnificent creation of God was removed from heaven and banished to the earth. Lucifer became Satan and was given the following titles and roles.

"God of This World" (or "god of this age")

II Corinthians 4:4 indicates that Satan is the major influence on the ideals, opinions, goals, hopes, and views of the majority of people. His influence also encompasses the world's philosophies, education, and commerce. The thoughts, ideas, speculations, and false religions of the world are under his control and have sprung from his lies and deceptions.

"Prince of the Power of the Air"

Ephesians 2:2 says, *"In which you used to live when you followed the ways of this world and the ruler of the kingdom of the air, the spirit who is now at work in those who are disobedient."* This tells us that the earth is currently under the rule of Satan. His power is exerted on humanity and tempts them to live in rebellion to God's plan for redemption.

"Prince of this World"

John 12:31 says, *"Now is the time for judgment on this world; now the prince of this world will be driven out."*

These titles and many more signify Satan's capabilities. To say, for example, that Satan is the "prince of the power of the air" is to signify that in some way he rules over the world and the people in it. This is not to say that he rules the world completely; God is still sovereign. But, it does mean that God, in His infinite wisdom, has allowed Satan to operate in this world within the boundaries God has set for him.

When the Bible says Satan has power over the world, we must remember that God has given him domain over *unbelievers* only. The unbeliever is trapped by Satan who has taken them captive to do his will as revealed in II Timothy 2:26, which says, *"and that they will come to their senses and escape from the trap of the devil, who has taken them captive to do his will."*

I John 5:19 goes on to say, *"... that the whole world is under the control of the evil one."*

Ephesians 2:1–2 says, *"As for you, you were dead in your transgressions and sins, in which you used to live when you followed the ways of this world and the ruler of the kingdom of the air, the spirit who is now at work in those who are disobedient."*

In 2 Corinthians 4:4, the unbeliever follows Satan's agenda: *"The god of this world has blinded the minds of unbelievers, so that they cannot see the light of the gospel of the glory of Christ."* Satan's scheme includes promoting false philosophies in the world. These are philosophies that blind the unbeliever to the truth of the Gospel.

When mankind sinned in Genesis 3, they put themselves under the brokenness of sin and the dominance of Satan. He is the source of all bondages and the one who keeps people in merciless slavery.

What caused God's plan for mankind to get off track?

Great News for Christ Followers

A new life begins! Christ Followers are no longer under the rule of Satan. The Apostle Paul wrote it like this: Jesus answered,

> *"Most assuredly, I say to you, unless one is born of water and the Spirit, he cannot enter the kingdom of*

> *God. That which is born of the flesh is flesh, and that which is born of the Spirit is spirit. Do not marvel that I said to you, 'You must be born again.'* (John 3:5-6 NET)

> *For He has rescued us from the dominion of darkness and brought us into the kingdom of the Son He loves, in whom we have redemption, the forgiveness of sins"* (Colossians 1:13 NET).

Paul also said, *"Therefore, if anyone is in Christ, he is a new creation; the old has gone [the dead spirit], the new has come [the indwelling Holy Spirit that makes us alive in Christ]"* (II Corinthians 5:17 NIV).

The final destination for Christ followers is described as the Promised Land. Similarly, Israel left Egypt (bondage) and headed for a land designed for them by God. He described it as a land flowing with milk and honey.

God never asked us to reform our lives. He said if we would give our lives to Him, He WILL transform us.

Take a good amount of time now and look at what Scripture says about those who are "born-again" followers of Jesus.

Who I Am in Jesus Christ

I am faithful. (Ephesians 1:1)

I am God's child. (John 1:12)

I have been justified. (Romans 5:1)

I am Christ's friend. (John 15:15)

I belong to God. (1 Corinthians 6:20)

I am a member of Christ's Body. (1 Corinthians 12:27)

I am assured all things work together for good. (Romans 8:28)

I have been established, anointed, and sealed by God. (2 Corinthians 1:21-22)

I am confident that God will perfect the work He has begun in me. (Philippians 1:6)

I am a citizen of heaven. (Philippians 3:20)

I am hidden with Christ in God. (Colossians 3:3)

I have not been given a spirit of fear. (2 Timothy 1:7)

I am born of God, and the evil one cannot touch me. (1 John 5:18)

I am blessed in the heavenly realms with every spiritual blessing. (Ephesians 1:3)

I am chosen before the creation of the world. (Ephesians 1:4, 11)

I am holy and blameless. (Ephesians 1:4)

I am adopted as his child. (Ephesians 1:5)

I am given God's glorious grace lavishly and without restriction. (Ephesians 1:5,8)

I am in Him. (Ephesians 1:7; 1 Corinthians 1:30)

I have redemption. (Ephesians 1:8)

I am forgiven. (Ephesians 1:8; Colossians 1:14)

I have purpose. (Ephesians 1:9 & 3:11)

I have hope. (Ephesians 1:12)

I am included. (Ephesians 1:13)

I am sealed with the promised Holy Spirit. (Ephesians 1:13)

I am a saint. (Ephesians 1:18)

I am alive with Christ. (Ephesians 2:5)

I am raised up with Christ. (Ephesians 2:6; Colossians 2:12)

I am seated with Christ in the heavenly realms. (Ephesians 2:6)

I have been shown the incomparable riches of God's grace. (Ephesians 2:7)

God has expressed His kindness to me. (Ephesians 2:7)

I have been brought near to God through Christ's blood. (Ephesians 2:13)

I have peace. (Ephesians 2:14)

I have access to the Father. (Ephesians 2:18)

I am a member of God's household. (Ephesians 2:19)

I am secure. (Ephesians 2:20)

I am a holy temple. (Ephesians 2:21; 1 Corinthians 6:19)

I am a dwelling for the Holy Spirit. (Ephesians 2:22)

I share in the promise of Christ Jesus. (Ephesians 3:6)

I am complete. (Ephesians 3:19)

I am chosen and dearly loved. (Colossians 3:12)

I am blameless. (I Corinthians 1:8)

I am set free. (Romans 8:2; John 8:32)

I am crucified with Christ. (Galatians 2:20

I am a light in the world. (Matthew 5:14)

What I Can Accomplish Through Him

I am salt and light of the earth. (Matthew 5:13-14)

I have been chosen and God desires me to bear fruit. (John 15:1,5)

I am a personal witness of Jesus Christ. (Acts 1:8)

I am God's coworker. (2 Corinthians 6:1)

I am a minister of reconciliation. (2 Corinthians 5:17-20)

I am God's workmanship. (Ephesians 2:10)

I have God's power working through me. (Ephesians 3:7)

I can approach God with freedom and confidence. (Ephesians 3:12)

I know there is a purpose for my sufferings. (Ephesians 3:13)

I can grasp how wide, long, high and deep is Christ's love. (Ephesians 3:18)

I can bring glory to God. (Ephesians 3:21)

I have been called. (Ephesians 4:1; 2 Timothy 1:9)

I can be humble, gentle, patient, and lovingly tolerant of others. (Ephesians 4:2)

I can mature spiritually. (Ephesians 4:15)

I can be certain of God's truths and the lifestyle to which He has called me. (Ephesians 4:17)

How I Have Been Transformed Through Jesus

I can have a new attitude and a new lifestyle. (Ephesians 4:21-32)
I can be kind and compassionate to others. (Ephesians 4:32)
I can forgive others. (Ephesians 4:32)
I am a light to others and can exhibit goodness, righteousness, and truth. (Ephesians 5:8-9)
I can understand what God's will is. (Ephesians 5:17)
I can give thanks for everything. (Ephesians 5:20)
I don't have to always have my own agenda. (Ephesians 5:21)
I can honor God through marriage. (Ephesians 5:22-33)
I can parent my children with composure. (Ephesians 6:4)
I can be strong. (Ephesians 6:10)
I have God's power. (Ephesians 6:10)
I can stand firm in the day of evil. (Ephesians 6:13)
I am dead to sin. (Romans 1:12)
I am not alone. (Hebrews 13:5)
I am growing. (Colossians 2:7)
I am His disciple. (John 13:15)
I am prayed for by Jesus Christ. (John 17:20-23)
I am united with other believers. (John 17:20-23)
I am not in want. (Philippians 4:19)
I possess the mind of Christ. (I Corinthians 2:16)
I am promised eternal life. (John 6:47)
I am promised a full life. (John 10:10)
I am victorious. (I John 5:4)
My heart and mind are protected with God's peace. (Philippians 4:7)
I am more than a conqueror. (Romans 8:37)
I am the righteousness of God. (2 Corinthians 5:21)
I am safe. (I John 5:18)
I am part of God's kingdom. (Revelation 1:6)
I am healed from sin. (I Peter 2:24)
I am no longer condemned. (Romans 8:1, 2)
I am not helpless. (Philippians 4:13)
I am overcoming. (I John 4:4)
I am persevering. (Philippians 3:14)

I am protected. (John 10:28)

I am born again. (I Peter 1:23)

I am a new creation. (2 Corinthians 5:17)

I am delivered. (Colossians 1:13)

I am redeemed from the curse of the Law. (Galatians 3:13)

I am qualified to share in His inheritance. (Colossians 1:12)

I am victorious. (1 Corinthians 15:57)

Go back and look at the list of things Scripture says you are because you are a follower of Jesus. Now put those truths up against the issues (lies that Satan has placed in your life), which keep you from freedom.

Let's Talk or Think About It

- **Attempt to describe what the "Promised Land" looks like for a Christ Follower.**

- **From the Scriptures listed above, what truths of God reveal areas of your life that still wrestle against some deception of Satan?**

Remember, it is really important to get a good picture in your heart and mind about the abundance in which Jesus wants you to live. This picture of the "Promised Land" is vital to us on the spiritual journey from bondage to abundance.

As you enter the third section of this book, we will take a close look at THE JOURNEY that makes up the Christian life as we seek to follow our Redeemer to the Promised Land.

SECTION #3

The Journey

CHAPTER 9

"The Transformed Mind"

In this part of the journey, the Israelites have left their bondage in Egypt, exchanged a slave master (Pharaoh) for a redeemer (Moses), and are now a free people on their way to the Promised Land, where life is promised in abundance. It is truly wonderful that these people have made it so far and have experienced salvation and freedom.

But, one major problem remains.

> **The problem is that IN their minds, they still see themselves as slaves.**

They still hear the words of the slave masters in their minds. They have been trained by the bondage of their world to be nothing more than a slave. So although recently freed, they still have much to overcome in their own thoughts. To understand how slavery had defeated them, read how the Israelites responded to their first challenge.

Read Exodus 14:8–12

Israel didn't understand freedom. From this record of Israel's journey, a few things are blatantly clear about how slavery had conformed their minds. All that they knew and were accustomed to was a life of bondage. There is a constant sense of fear that accompanies slavery. The fear of abuse, the fear of displeasing the overseer, the fear of survival, and the fear of a future with no hope for improvement created a familiar companion in each slave. Israel was so trained in the parameters of slavery and bondage that at some points of their journey toward freedom, it seemed less scary for them to go back into slavery than to continue toward freedom. The abuse and training in slavery convinced Israel that the power of their old slave masters was stronger than the power of their God.

Unless this type of thinking was changed, Israel had no chance to walk in freedom. They would be doomed to return to their life of bondage and slavery.

The need to overcome an old mindset is revealed by Mary. Mary was a young, highly trained professional who worked in the health care industry as a nurse. She had been raised in a Christ-honoring home and had all of the opportunities necessary for living in the freedom that Jesus offers. In her late teenage years, Mary became pregnant out of wedlock, which brought a lot of shame and condemnation into her life. To deal with the pain of this shame, she turned to drugs and alcohol to numb her failures. The problem with this was that she became emotionally and physically addicted to the drugs. Being in the health care profession, she had the ability to get a hold of prescription painkillers easily. For a few years, Mary was able to maintain stability by staying just sober enough to make it through her work, but high enough to dull the pain she felt and the fear that terrorized her. In the evening, alcohol would be added to the painkillers until Mary found herself unconscious in an attempt to find some rest.

As all slave masters do, her bondage to drugs and alcohol intensified and began to control her. Mary reached the point that she was unable to care for her child. Her ability to function in her work was beginning to shake apart as well.

Suspicions increased at work as painkillers came up missing. Rumors flew as coworkers talked about Mary's DUIs, the neglect of her child, and the severe deterioration of Mary's body. At this point, Mary's slave master was destroying her life.

When the ability to hide the addiction failed, Mary's family stepped in to help. In partnership with a church, Mary consented to go to a Teen Challenge program, which leads young adults through a Christ-centered recovery program. The Teen Challenge program understands bondages and the journey that is required to lead a person into freedom.

Mary went through the entire program, and under the supervision and training of the Teen Challenge staff, she prospered. She was able to go through detoxification and a thorough process to begin retraining her thinking. But, as soon as she was released from the program, the fear of freedom and the challenges of her life came back much like Pharaoh came after Israel when they first left bondage. Mary ran back into slavery. The familiarity of slavery was more comfortable than the journey to freedom. Mary is back under her slave masters, and her life is apparently in a merciless bondage. There is always hope in Christ, but at this moment, Mary lives in a very sad place of slavery.

What Satanic deceptions have been the hardest for you to overcome?

How have those deceptions hurt and hindered your life?

What Do We Do With This Reality?

The greatest answer to the temptation that pushes us to go back into bondage is found in the writings of the Apostle Paul.

> *Do not conform any longer to the pattern of this world, but be transformed by the renewing of your mind. Then you will be able to test and approve what God's will is—His good, pleasing and perfect will.* (Romans 12:2 NIV)

Jesus helped us understand the primary work of Satan when He said, *"He was a murderer from the beginning, not holding to the truth, for there is not truth in him. When he lies, he speaks his native language, for he is a liar and the father of lies."* (John 8:44 NIV)

To overcome the lies that have been planted in our mind by Satan and his slave masters, we must go back to a truth found in Chapter 3.

- WORDS become IDEAS
- IDEAS become BELIEF
- BELIEF becomes ACTION

Step 1: Do Not Be Conformed

Paul said, *"Do not conform any longer to the pattern of this world."*

Here, we must begin to identify the deceptions that were planted in our minds while we were in slavery. The deceptions that were placed in our minds have grown over the years to form a stronghold. A stronghold is a complex structure of thought that establishes a false thinking pattern, corrupting God's original design for our lives.

Scripture gives us guidelines on how to identify the deceptions that have been planted in our minds.

IDENTIFY A SATANIC DECEPTION

- **When the deceptions steal, kill, or destroy.** Scripture reveals this truth when it says, *"The thief [messenger of Satan] comes only to steal and kill and destroy"* (John 10:10 NIV).

  A word empowered by the demonic influence can be spoken into a life by a loved one, a friend, or an authority figure that wounds in a way that leaves an identifying scar on our view of life. It is heard when a father speaks a curse, like Mike's story in Chapter 2. When his father said, "You are lazy and will never amount to anything." An emotional wound can occur when a mother says, "You are ugly and no one will ever want to marry you." Casual words spoken in frustration, anger, or ignorance can end up stealing, killing, and destroying.

- **When God's Word is hard to understand.** *"When anyone hears the word about the kingdom and does not understand it, the evil one comes* *and snatches what was sown in his heart; this is the seed sown along the path."*(Matthew 13:19 NET)

The Word of God is truth. The principles, the promises, and the instructions of God through the Holy Scripture are like a light that dispels the darkness. Satan attempts to keep people from hearing the Word of God. He uses misinformation to make people think that God's Word is just a list of "do's and don'ts" that are meant to ruin their fun. Satan also uses confusion to cause people to be quickly frustrated as they attempt to search God's Word for help.

- **When condemnation is spoken.** *"For God did not send his Son into the world to condemn the world, but that the world should be saved through him."*(John 3:17 NET)

From my view, there is a spirit of religion that is demonically empowered. It is neither based on a relationship with Jesus nor guided by His Word. It is a spiritually superior feeling of a religious person over someone they consider lesser than themselves. And in this position, words of self-righteous judgment are spoken that place people under condemnation. Paul clarified the importance of Godly love in the life of a Christ follower.

- **When you have been cursed.** *"The tongue has the power of life and death, and those who love it will eat its fruit."* (Proverbs 18:21 NIV)

This occurs when a destructive word has been spoken into your life that causes you to have a warped view of yourself. Satan's plan is to define you by his lies and curses so that you never find God and never find the redemption He has planned for your life and family.

- **When your values are based on fear.** *"When he [Satan] lies, he speaks his native language, for he is a liar and the father of lies."* (John 8:44 NIV)

I believe that the main power Satan uses to destroy is fear. He uses many different tools to lead us away from the Lord, but fear is his specialty.

- **When you have given in to temptation to sin.** *"Each one is tempted when, by his own evil desire, he is dragged away and enticed. Then, after desire had conceived, it gives birth to sin; and sin, when it is full grown, gives birth to death."* (James 1:14 NIV)

There is a clear progression in this passage that reveals the steps to death. First, we are tempted by power, position, prestige, sexual fulfillment, and greed. Second, that desire drags us toward sin. Third, sin gives birth to death. So it is our sin that destroys our life, and there is no way to be made right with God except through the substitute payment for our sins by Jesus.

- **When there is demonic oppression.** *"Jesus rebuked the demon, and it came out of the boy, and he was healed from that moment."* (Matthew 17:18 NIV)

I am fully aware that in our day of scientific discovery, many people have decided there is no real evil spiritual world. It is my observation that the demonic is always at work seeking to steal from us, kill us, and destroy God's design for our lives.

- **When confusion reigns.** *"For God is not a God of confusion but of peace."* (I Corinthians 14:33 ESV)

Being pressured, stressed, and pushed many times causes us to make decisions in the middle of confusion. This practice almost guarantees failure.

- **When being self-righteous.** *"Jesus said to them, 'Be on your guard against the yeast of the Pharisees and Sadducees.'"* (Matthew 16:6 NIV).

Pharisees and Sadducees represent the religious legalists, those who believe they are better than others because they are rule keepers. But the reality is that self-righteousness is an outward show to cover an inward spiritual deadness.

- **When controlled by flesh desires.** *"Do not love the world or the things in the world. If anyone loves the world, the love of the Father is not in him. For all that is in the world—the desires of the flesh and the desires of the eyes and pride in possession—is not from the Father but is from the world. And the world is passing away along with its desires, but whoever does the will of God abides forever."* (I John 2:15–17 ESV)

For many years in America, we have emphasized the worship of materialism: the thought that the purpose of life is to pursue material prosperity at the expense of our spirits, which are dead in trespass and sin.

These are the things that cause us to be conformed to the pattern of this world. But there is a second step that begins to move us toward life.

Step 2: BE TRANSFORMED

Paul said, *"Be transformed by the renewing of your mind."* (Romans 12:2 NIV)

This is the process whereby we begin to replace the lies of Satan with the truths of God's Word. Darkness is replaced by light, and deception is replaced by truth. There are many potential steps toward renewing your mind, but here are a few of the most important tools that will help you with this transformation.

- *Clarity and Direction*

  "Your Word is a lamp unto my feet and a light for my path."
  (Psalm 119:105 NIV)

This "Word" is the Word of God as revealed through Scripture. As we spend time in God's Word in a daily reading, as we study God's Word personally and in groups, and as the Holy Spirit opens our understanding to His truth, enlightenment enters our life more and more. Each time this occurs, more light and truth are revealed and more darkness and confusion are removed.

- ***Focus on Truth***

> *Jesus told him, "I am the way, the truth, and the life. No one can come to the Father except through me.*(John 14:6 NLT)

A study of the prophecies in the books of Daniel and Revelation reveals that there will be an increase of deception as the world nears its close. Daniel says, "*The saints will be handed over to him [the one world ruler] for a time, times, and half a time*" (Daniel 7:25 NIV) This suggests that increasing persecution will develop toward those who follow Jesus. Deception will increase, and persecution will become more aggressive because Jesus is truth. Since Satan is the opposite of Jesus, he is the great deceiver, and Jesus and His followers become his primary target.

- ***Dwell in God's Word***

> "*Let the Word of Christ dwell in you richly as you teach and admonish one another with all wisdom.*" (Colossians 3:16 NIV)

This is the importance of constant time in God's Word. Why?

**The wisdom of God Word leads to an abundant
life and preparation for eternity.**

- ***Be Faithful in a Bible-Believing Church***

> *All the believers devoted themselves to the apostles' teaching, and to fellowship, and to sharing in meals (including the Lord's Supper), and to prayer.*(Acts 2:42 NLT)

I have found that isolated Christ followers soon become targets of the enemy. The lone Christian is not as strong as a Christian who walks in fellowship with other believers because the people of God offer faithful friendship, Godly counsel, and Biblical instruction that helps us stay strong in the Lord.

- **Grow in Faith to Overcome Fear**

> *"Faith comes from hearing the message, and the message is heard through the Word of God"* (Romans 10:17 NIV).

If you wish to walk in true victory, then you must stand on God's Word, which leads to righteousness. The transformed mind takes quite a while to develop because the process has to be a determined effort. This is called discipleship. A disciple is a student. For true Christ followers, the teacher is Jesus Christ. Jesus said He would lead us into all truth.

Step 3: SEEK GOD'S WILL

Paul said, *"Then you will be able to test and approve what God's will is—His good, pleasing and perfect will."* (Romans 12:2 NIV)

Back in Chapter 3, we looked at how a deception is implanted that brings a life into bondage. The third step of transformation is accomplished by taking God's Word into your life in the same way.

- WORDS become IDEAS: In this step, God's Word is read and considered until it begins to shape your IDEAS.

- IDEAS become BELIEF: As you consider God's truths, you begin to form your Kingdom-of-God-minded belief system.

- BELIEF becomes ACTION: When your Scripture-based belief drives your actions, you begin to live as a representative of God.

Therefore, to begin your life of faith, I encourage the following Scriptures as a good starting point for transformation.

- **Prepare Your Mind for Action**

> *"Therefore, preparing your minds for action, and being sober-minded, set your hope fully on the grace that will be brought to you at the revelation of Jesus Christ"* (I Peter 11:12 ESV)

As we have carefully discussed, there is a war of thoughts that bombard our thinking. Some of the thoughts are from our fleshly desires and others are from demonic insertion. Therefore the only way to become stable an to live in Godly peace is to bring our thoughts captive to God's Word.

- **Begin Living as a New Creation**

> *"Therefore, if anyone is in Christ, he is a new creation; the old has gone, the new has come."* (II Corinthians 5:17 NIV)

This is the primary purpose for this book. The purpose is to help us get rid of the old way of life and thinking that kept us in bondage. Because the God reality is that when we accept Jesus into our life as the forgiver of our sin, He also comes to us in the power of His Holy Spirit and we are made new.

- *Start Believing in Your God-Given Purpose*

"There are different kinds of spiritual gifts, but the same Spirit is the source of them all. There are different kinds of service, but we serve the same Lord. God works in different ways, but it is the same God who does the work in all of us." (I Corinthians 12:4–6 NLT) Another exciting concept for Christ followers is that when we receive the Lord into our life He enters us bringing spiritual gifts. These gifts allow us to serve Him and function in the power of His Kingdom.

- *Advance Toward Your Life of Abundance*

Jesus said, *"I have come that they may have life, and have it to the full."* (John 10:10b NIV)

The following is a tool that may be of help to you as you seek to identify God's voice in the midst of the many loud voices that are attempting to maintain your attention.

GOD'S VOICE	SATAN'S VOICE
Stills you	Rushes you
Leads you	Pushes you
Reassures you	Frightens you
Enlightens you	Confuses you
Encourages you	Discourages you
Comforts you	Worries you
Calms you	Obsesses you
Convicts you	Condemns you

When we take the leap of faith and receive Jesus as the forgiver of our sins and the controller of our lives, He takes our spirit that once was empty and dead due to sin and failure and makes it "new" by His Holy Spirit. God now dwells within you. This is where Scripture says, *"He is a new creation; the old has gone, the new has come."* (II Corinthians 5:17 NIV)

The most marvelous news on planet Earth is that a lost and broken person can be found, forgiven, and healed by the Lord Jesus Christ.

Let's Talk or Think About It

As you list the Satanic deceptions, what Word (TRUTH) of God have you found that has helped you to be transformed above those lies?

The Satanic Lie:
The Scriptural Truth:

The Satanic Lie:
The Scriptural Truth:

The Satanic Lie:
The Scriptural Truth:

If you are still in bondage to a deception or a curse, share with your small group for prayer and scriptural counsel or meet with your Pastor so that you can find God's truth that will set you free.

CHAPTER 10

"Overcoming Fear With Faith"

The primary power of Satan's demonic world is *intimidation and fear.*

Please don't underestimate the power that is found in fear. Psychologists suggest that the influence of fear causes us to run in one of two directions: fight or flight. FLIGHT is the response in us to flee from a scary situation. We choose to run away from the problem, to avoid it, or to deny it. The second potential path is FIGHT. If we choose this path, fear releases adrenaline that prompts us to stand and fight or to strike back against that which is causing our fear.

As Israel left Egypt, they had several opportunities for fear. Many of their experiences provoke the same fears that we may face.

- **The Fear of Being Overtaken By Past Slave Masters (Bondage)**

Read Exodus 14:9–12

THE FAITH RESPONSE: Trust God to make a way of escape and know that God desires freedom for His people.

Continue in Exodus 14:13

God supernaturally provided a way of escape by parting the Red Sea. (see Exodus 14:13–31)

- **The Fear of Life's Bitter Circumstances**

Read Exodus 15:22–24

THE FAITH RESPONSE: God provides a plan found within each life crisis that will turn the bitterness into sweetness if we listen and obey His voice.

Continue in Exodus 15:25–26

- **The Fear of Not Having Enough Food**

> *"Then the whole community of Israel set out from Elim and journeyed into the wilderness of Sin,[a] between Elim and Mount Sinai. They arrived there on the fifteenth day of the second month, one month after leaving the land of Egypt. There, too, the whole community of Israel complained about Moses and Aaron.*
>
> *"If only the Lord had killed us back in Egypt," they moaned. "There we sat around pots filled with meat and ate all the bread we wanted. But now you have brought us into this wilderness to starve us all to death."* (Exodus 16:1–3 NLT)

THE FAITH RESPONSE: God promises to provide for our needs according to His riches in heaven. Our existence may be on Manna, God's daily provision, until we are ready to cross over the Jordan (river of hindrance) into God's Promised Land. Manna is a test to see if we will obey Him by bringing the first tenth of our production to Him in worship. *"I will rain down bread from heaven [Manna] for you. The people are to go out each day and gather enough for that day. In this way, I will test them and see whether they will follow my instructions."* (Exodus 16:4 NIV)

- **The Fear of Being Overtaken By an Enemy**

Read Exodus 17:8–9

THE FAITH RESPONSE: Stay in fellowship with other believers, who will help us maintain victory.

Read Exodus 17:11–12

Victory is always God's plan for His people. As Moses lifted his staff, Israel would win in the battle. When his hand lowered, the enemy began to win. So, others came alongside Moses to hold his hands in a victorious position. Satan likes to isolate us and there he can weaken us and makes us vulnerable to his stealing, killing, and destroying. We need to be in fellowship with other believers who will help to keep us in a victory position when we find ourselves in times of weakness or fatigue.

- **The Fear of Conquering**

The greatest fear came as God asked his people to become conquerors instead of simple followers.

> *Now they departed and came back to Moses and Aaron and all the congregation of the children of Israel in the Wilderness of Paran, at Kadesh; they brought back word to them and to all the congregation, and showed them the fruit of the land. Then they told him, and said: "We went to the land where you sent us. It truly flows with milk and honey, and this is its fruit. Nevertheless the people who dwell in the land are strong; the cities are fortified and very large; moreover we saw the descendants of Anak there. The Amalekites dwell in the land of the South; the Hittites, the Jebusites, and the Amorites dwell in the mountains; and the Canaanites dwell by the sea and along the banks of the Jordan."*

> *Then Caleb quieted the people before Moses, and said, "Let us go up at once and take possession, for we are well able to overcome it."*
>
> *But the men who had gone up with him said, "We are not able to go up against the people, for they are stronger than we." And they gave the children of Israel a bad report of the land which they had spied out, saying, "The land through which we have gone as spies is a land that devours its inhabitants, and all the people whom we saw in it are men of great stature. There we saw the giants[a] (the descendants of Anak came from the giants); and we were like grasshoppers in our own sight, and so we were in their sight." (Numbers 13:26–33 NKJV)*

THE FAITH RESPONSE: Joshua and Caleb show us how to advance spiritually. They saw the same obstacles, fears, and giants in the land as the others. But, they chose to believe God and His Word over the intimidation of the enemy.

> *But Joshua the son of Nun and Caleb the son of Jephunneh, who were among those who had spied out the land, tore their clothes; 7 and they spoke to all the congregation of the children of Israel, saying: "The land we passed through to spy out is an exceedingly good land. 8 If the Lord delights in us, then He will bring us into this land and give it to us, 'a land which flows with milk and honey.'[a] 9 Only do not rebel against the Lord, nor fear the people of the land, for they are our bread; their protection has departed from them, and the Lord is with us. Do not fear them." (Numbers 14:6-9 NKJV)*

My largest fear faced me when the church I pastored went through a season of pruning that I shared with you in Chapter 5. As the church went through this season, we lost over 13 key families, and along with this pruning came all of the overwhelming losses that happen with a devastating event. I fell into a very deep, dark, painful, and scary pit. The pit was filled with poison-tipped spikes of failure, rejection, shattered dreams, lost friendships, disillusionment, insecurity, and stress... stress... stress! **Did I mention that it was stressful?** It was so poisonous that my autoimmune system started attacking my kidneys and did severe damage that put me in the hospital a couple of times during this period. I felt like I had *failed* in my life calling. I felt like I had *failed* my family. I felt like I had *failed* the church. And, probably the biggest pain was that I felt like I had FAILED THE LORD!

In the explosion of this event, I was blown apart and what was revealed in me was a lot of fear. When I evaluated the source of the fear, I came to see that I had a great fear of failure. What I had a harder time realizing was that I was doing a lot of what I would call "God's Work" to prove that I was of value. I wanted to prove that I was worth something and the only way that I could do this was to be successful in the eyes of men. (Did I really just say that out loud?)

When broken down completely, it was plain to see that my fear of failure was simply a result of PRIDE.

I found that when pride remains, it comes carrying a whole host of self-protective paper shields. These paper shields can be labeled in many different ways coming in many different forms. They may look like:

1. Striving
2. Pressure
3. Competing
4. Acting like a slave master
5. All work and no rest
6. All stress and no joy
7. All hiding and no transparency
8. You may add to this list if you have struggled with pride in your life as well.

What fear(s) is/are your biggest enemy that hinders you from walking in victory?

So how DO WE overcome the power of fear in our life?

The Shield of Faith

In Ephesians 6:10–18, the Apostle Paul tells us about our very real spiritual battles and the enemies that we must combat. In this section of Scripture, there is a piece of battle armor that sticks out as you read it. It says, ***"And above all else, take up the SHIELD OF FAITH,*** *with which you can extinguish all the flaming arrows [temptations, doubt, fear] of the evil one"* (Ephesians 6:16 KJV)

So it is <u>faith</u> in the form of a <u>shield</u> that gives us victory over the greatest tool of our enemy. And the greatest tool of our enemy is fear. Shields are heavy, bulky, uncomfortable, not very fashion sensitive, and must be picked up as we enter war or when we are vulnerable to attack. As you look at all of the equipment for warfare that Paul talks about, notice that there is no protection from the back. This means we are to never run from the battle. Running only exposes our backside.

We are to stand strong facing the enemy in the might of the Lord with armor on and shield in place.

I read a story in college that has always stuck with me about the reality of war and those who take it seriously. The story is about the Spartans. The Spartans were a warring people. They came to own the principle that, "Freedom comes from a strong defense system." It had become so ingrained into their psyche and culture that if a male child was born into a Spartan family that was sickly or handicapped, they would take the baby out on a hill and leave it to die. They did this because they had a belief that "if the child is not worthy of being a warrior, it is not worthy of life."

Although extreme and savage, it did represent their understanding of the necessity of strength for war. At the age of seven, sons that were born healthy and whole were sent from the home to the Spartan military training school. Until the age of twenty, these young men studied warfare. They were taught to understand and use weapons of war. They studied war strategies. They trained mentally and physically to be their strongest. For thirteen years, they lived with warriors, ate with warriors, trained with warriors, and had off times with warriors. Before they were twenty, they were strong, buff, fighting machines.

Sparta was so proud of their army that they were able to boast, "We do not have walls of defense around our city because our men are our walls." Strong, trained, equipped, and committed warriors created a defense around this city that no enemy would dare to test.

The "shield of faith" that the Apostle Paul talked about connects to the story of a twenty-year-old Spartan when he goes out to face his first battle. On the morning of the battle, the mother of the warrior would bring the shield that had been made for her son or she would bring her son the shield that his father had used. If it was the father's shield, it was given because the father had been killed in battle; thus, it was the son's honor to carry the shield. This was a family honor presentation that was formal and highly respected. As the family presented the shield to the son he would speak the following oath:

> *This is my shield,*
> *I bear it before me in battle,*
> *But it is not mine alone.*
> *It protects my brother on my left.*
> *It protects my city.*
> *I will never let my brother out of its shadow*
> *Nor my city out of its shelter.*
> *I will die with my shield before me*
> *Facing the enemy.*

After reciting the Warrior's Creed, the son would pick up the shield as the mother would lean in and whisper these words to her son: "Above all, honor this shield. Either bring this shield back or be brought back on this shield."

The shield represents all that we believe in. For the true Christ follower, spiritual warfare is a daily reality. Our battle is not just for ourselves. It is for our brothers on the left and on the right; it is for our family; it is for our church; it is for our city; it is for our nation. Our belief about God and who He is makes up the structure of our shield. I must know beyond all doubt who God is so that when the battle is raging, I can turn to the beliefs carved into my shield of faith.

- God is good.
- God is all-powerful.
- God is all knowing.
- God is sovereign.
- God's Son Jesus is the forgiver of my sin.
- God's Holy Spirit lives within me to guide, equip, and strengthen me for victory.
- I can do all things through Christ who gives me strength.

This shield will guard me. This shield will catch and put out the fiery arrows of the enemy. This shield, when put together with my brothers on my left and right, will create an impenetrable guard against the enemy. Above all else, Honor the Shield!

If your shield was engraved with your belief system, what would it say?

I believe that...

I believe that...

I believe that...

I believe that...

I believe that...

Do you have a scriptural truth your belief system is based upon? Can you match a scriptural truth to each of your belief statements listed above?

The mother's challenge was that the definition of the son's life would be determined by what he did with his shield. "Hero" or "Coward" will be his epitaph based on what he did with his shield. As true Christ followers, we must likewise grip our shield of faith "hard" in the time of battle because those who do not, will run in the face of the enemy. Here are the coward's virtues:

- They follow personalities instead of God.
- They seek inspiring experiences instead of being trained for warfare.
- They easily join the ranks of the disgruntled.
- They blame God when their shield folds due to unbelief.
- They run from battle.
- They seek fellowship with a community of cowards.

Our challenge as the Christ follower is the same one the Spartan mother gives to her son. "Either bring this shield back or be brought back on this shield."

Why do you believe that this shield of faith is important to your ability to live in victory over fear?

This position reminds me of the Shadrach, Meshach, and Abednego story found in Daniel, chapter 3. Their King (government) started demanding loyalty and worship to the point that if people chose to worship God, they were threatened with death. Their punishment was to burn and die in a fiery furnace. It was in the face of this level of intimidation that these three God-fearing boys made a statement about their shield.

Read Daniel 3:17–18

Even if it is not God's plan to rescue me in this current battle, I will die on my belief in Him and will not be swayed. If death is what I face, then carry me home on my shield. Above all else, pick up the shield of faith.

Why is it important that we partner with fellow spiritual warriors who have a similar shield of faith (belief system) and are fully committed to the cause of Christ?

This position of belief created a strong Shield of Faith for these three young men. The Bible story tells us that God intervened in this fiery test and these boys walked out of the furnace *unscorched*! The power of God was undeniable.

Let's Talk or Think About It

- **What is the belief system that your shield is made of? What are the core beliefs that you will live by or die by?**

- **Is your shield strong enough to protect you and your loved ones in the time of battle? Are you committed enough to stand in the face of overwhelming odds?**

- **Does your faith protect you from the arrows of fear?**

As we close this chapter, please allow me to challenge you one more time with the Spartan war command.

HONOR THE SHIELD... EITHER BRING THIS SHIELD BACK... OR BE BROUGHT BACK ON THIS SHIELD!

CHAPTER 11

"The Road Less Traveled"

Here is a riddle for you:

> *It happens hundreds of times each day.*
>
> *It happens with little consequence at times. It happens with life altering effects at times.*
>
> *The cumulative effect of these determines the quality of your life. To avoid one of these, is to make one of these.*
>
> *What is it?*

The answer to the riddle is "a decision."

Pick a significant decision from this past week. Did you decide that issue based on FAITH in God and His Word or did FEAR direct your decision?

- **If it was based on faith, what Word, principle, or promise of God did you stand upon?**
- **If it was based on fear, what consequences do you see coming because of that decision?**

Many times, a point of decision gives two basic options.

Read Matthew 7:13–14, answer the following:

- **Who or what do you think is the narrow gate? Why?**
- **What do you think is the wide gate that leads to destruction? Why?**
- **Why do many enter through the wide gate?**
- **Why does Jesus say the small gate and narrow road leads to life?**
- **Why do you think only a few find it?**

Let me propose a concept around this option Jesus calls "The Wide Gate and Broad Road".

Option #1: The Wide Gate and Broad Road of Fear

Using Israel as an example, we can see the journey from slavery to abundance, but there is also a piece of this story that shows what happens when a road of fear is chosen.

The choice between a *road of fear* and a *road of faith* was clearly observed as Israel came to the border of the land of promise. Twelve spies were chosen: one from each of the tribes that made up the Jewish cultural structure. This team of twelve was given the assignment to explore. On this exploration, they were to find out what the land was like and to see if the people who lived there were strong or weak. They were to find out if there were few or many people, and if their cities were walled or fortified. How was the soil? Was it fertile or poor? Were there trees on it? The twelve went on their covert journey, and after a forty-day exploration, they came back with this report.

Read Numbers 13:26–28

The twelve spies saw the proof of the land God promised Israel. But, along with the great benefits of the land, the spies also saw things that caused them fear. They saw that the inhabitants of the land were powerful. They discovered that the cities there were fortified and large. Then to top off the hindrances, they also discovered that there were giants in the land. As the twelve spies came back, there were two different reports given.

The FAITH Report

The minority report was held by two of the twelve spies, Joshua and Caleb.

> *"Then Caleb silenced the people before Moses and said, "We should go up and take possession of the land, for we can certainly do it."* (Numbers 13:30 NIV)

The FEAR Report

Then the majority of the spies brought their report and opinion.

> *"But the people who live there are powerful, and the cities are fortified and very large. We even saw descendants of Anak there... we seemed like grasshoppers in our own eyes, and we looked the same to them."* (Numbers 13:28 & 33b)

Read Numbers 13:27–33

Because of this report from the majority of the spies, the people who were so close to moving into the land God promised them decided to turn left and choose the road of fear. This is what their decision looked like:

Read Numbers 14:2–4

Let's take a moment and look at what fear does when we let it influence our decisions.

- **Fear Hides the Presence, Power, and Promise of God**

When Israel saw the very real challenges that stood between them and the land God had promised them, the challenges consumed their minds with fear. All they could see were giants and large fortified cities. In other words, their problems were so big that they were paralyzed with fear.

Israel had forgotten the promise that God had given them through Moses.

> *Therefore say to the Israelites: "I Am the Lord, and I will bring you out from under the yoke of the Egyptians. I will free you from being slaves to them, and I will redeem you with an outstretched arm and with mighty acts of judgment. I will take you as My own people, and I will be your God. They you will know that I am the Lord your God, who brought you out from under the yoke of the Egyptians.* **And I will bring you to the land I swore with uplifted hand to give to Abraham, to Isaac, and to Jacob. I will give it to you as a possession.** *I am the Lord."* (Exodus 6:6–8 NIV)

- **Fearfully Made Decisions Have Painful Consequences**

Israel chose fear and turned left at the point of decision. A fear decision comes with very real consequences, especially when we allow our life to be controlled by this fear. For Israel, the result was not pleasant.

Read Numbers 14:27–34

- **Fear Has a False God**

In Matthew, Jesus said, *"No one can serve two masters. Either he will hate the one and love the other, or he will hold to the one and despise the other. You cannot serve both God and Mammon."* (Matthew 6:24 KJV)

Based on this word from Jesus, there are two possible masters for our lives. One master is God and this is chosen by faith. The other god is Mammon and it is chosen by fear.

The word **mammon** in the original language is *"mamonas"* of Chaldean origin, and it means confidence or wealth personified. An example of this would be avarice. **Avarice** means an insatiable greed for riches—inordinate or miserly desire to gain and horde wealth.

**When *fear* is the motivator in a decision, we are really
shifting our position to come under the god of fear.**

When you add fear to mankind's fallen nature, an insatiable desire to horde
wealth physically and especially spiritually is in reality an effort to DEIFY
ONESELF. This goes all the way back to the Garden of Eden, where Satan
tempted Eve with the words, *"You will be like God."*

When fear rules, the driving force of our life is hoarding wealth, and
we buy into a spirituality that keeps ourselves as priority instead of the
Lordship of Jesus. This means that we want to be in control of our own
lives. If we find ourselves wanting to control every aspect of our lives and
the lives of those around us, there is a good chance the motivator is fear.

Let's go back and read Numbers 13:27–33, where 10 of the 12 Jewish spies
made their decision based upon fear.

What are the consequences of decisions based upon fear?

Option #2 The Road of Faith

There is a very different road we can take at every point of decision. We
do not have to choose the road of fear because God's Word says, *"God has
not given us a spirit of fear; but of power, and of love, and a sound mind."*
(II Timothy 1:7 KJV)

Therefore, as we come to one of the many points of decision in our lives,
we can simply take a breath, seek the will of God in prayer, find scriptures
that give guidance on the subject, and then choose the road of faith.

Faith is simply seeing that our God is bigger than our current challenges.

Caleb and Joshua held this position. They were the only two of the twelve
spies who went in to inspect the land of promise and came back still
believing what God had promised. When they came back, they had seen
the same giants and the same fortified cities, yet their response was opposite

of the other ten. The difference occurred because Caleb and Joshua chose to see the greatness and superior strength of their God instead of being overwhelmed with the obstacles before them.

This is the difference between fear and faith:

- **Fear** focuses on the challenge, difficulty, and hindrance.
- **Faith** focuses on God and His unlimited ability.

There are several benefits to choosing faith when we are faced with a decision. Faith brings deliverance. Faith brings peace. Faith brings hope into the crisis.

Benefits of choosing Faith

- **Faith Brings Deliverance**

If we go back to the story of the Israelites after they had chosen fear, we find them complaining against their circumstances, their leader, and even God. They began making plans to return back to their slavery. Moses, their leader, stood up in the face of their fear and said, *"Do not be afraid. Stand firm and you will see the deliverance the Lord will bring you today. The Egyptians [slave masters] you see today you will never see again. The Lord will fight for you; you need only to be still"* (Exodus 14:13–14 NIV). Some points of emphasis we can take away from this illustration are as follows:

Stand Firm and Do Not Run

The first action to take if you are going to choose faith when you face a decision is to stand firm and simply stand in faith. God does most of the fighting for us when we face strong forces and do not run.

Do Not Be Impressed With the Challenge

When Israel faced their first challenge, they came face to face with a large, fortified city, Jericho that appeared impregnable. The road to victory came by not being impressed with the size and strength of their enemy, but instead listening to the Word and will of God. By simply being obedient to His will and trusting His power, victory was theirs.

Focus on the Superiority of God

This is what God said to Israel as they faced their first challenge when entering the land of promise: *"Then the Lord said to Joshua, 'See I have delivered Jericho into your hands, along with its king and its fighting men.'"* (Joshua 6:2 NIV) When we focus our attention on the message, character, power, and wisdom of our God, our faith increases. As faith increases, the intimidation of the challenge decreases.

Listen and Obey the Word of God

"March around the city once with all the armed men. Do this for six days. Have seven priests carry trumpets of rams' horns in front of the ark. On the seventh day, march around the city seven times, with the priests blowing the trumpets. When you hear them, sound a long blast on the trumpets, have all the people give a loud shout; then the wall of the city will collapse and the people will go up, every man straight in." (Joshua 6:3–5 NIV)

Experience the Victory

As Israel obeyed this unusual command of God, they saw the impossible happen. The walls of the Jericho literally crumbled, allowing each Israelite to go in and claim the city for the Lord. When God works on our behalf, our enemy and hindrance collapse. After the Lord moves, all we have to do is to go in and claim the new territory for God.

• **Faith Brings Peace**

In the midst of a challenge or crisis, the intensity and volume of voices and messages we receive seem to increase. *"You should do this!"* *"You should do that!"* *"You need to stop doing this!"* *"You need to stop doing that!"* *"What if you did this?"* *"I wonder why this happened?"* *"What did I do wrong?"* *"Is God punishing me?"* *"Is there even a God?"* These thoughts and questions start spinning around in our head and they turn into tornados of thoughts, circling and forever repeating in our mind. They are so pervasive that we can't find rest or peace. Instead, fatigue is all we can feel.

In the midst of this type of chaos, God's Word rings a bell of clarity. The Bible has a word for any situation, and when we find His Word for our situation, that Word brings a sense of stability and peace. Jesus gave us an example when He spoke to the storm on the Sea of Galilee. The word says, *"And he awoke and rebuked the wind and said to the sea, 'Peace! Be still!' And the wind ceased, and there was a great calm"* (Mark 4:39 ESV)

- **Faith Brings Hope**

There are unlimited scenarios in life that can cause us to find ourselves on a trash heap of hopelessness. The boss says, "I have to lay you off." The doctor says, "It is cancer." The banker tells you, "Foreclosure on your house is your only way out of this because your income just doesn't meet your needs." Your spouse breaks the news, "I'm done with you and our marriage." You lose someone you love and grief grips your heart. Right behind these setbacks comes the worst pain of all - hopelessness.

Another way to look at the power of hopelessness is to compare it to darkness.

The greater the depth of hopelessness the darker the condition

This kind of darkness in a person's soul carries a terrifying emptiness and a pain that becomes unbearable. If darkness resembles hopelessness, then light represents hope. The key to overcoming darkness is the addition of light. "Your word is a lamp to my feet and a light for my path." (Psalm 119:105 NIV)

Hope comes from God's Word and His Spirit's presence in our life. The Apostle Paul said it like this, *"Faith comes from hearing the message, and the message is heard through the Word of Christ."* (Romans 10:17 NIV)

- **Faith Brings God into the Crisis**

At the bottom of our crisis, we will find that God is enough. When our focus turns from the chaos of the crisis and the largeness of our challenge toward the goodness of our God, something begins to change. When we choose to look at His infinite wisdom and His unequalled power, our eyes automatically turn from our challenge and instead lock in on God. When that happens, it's not long before we realize <u>God Is Enough</u>!

As we said at the beginning of this chapter, we face hundreds of decisions each day. Have you ever stopped long enough in each decision of the day to ask this question: "Am I deciding on this issue by FAITH in God and His Word or by FEAR?" It is a worthwhile question. If it is asked sincerely and answered in faith, God guides our decisions; then our life will truly be blessed. Messy consequences that occur when fear leads us to make foolish decisions will no longer hound our life.

Reconsider what Jesus said: *"Enter through the narrow gate. For wide is the gate and broad is the road that leads to destruction, and many enter through it. But small is the gate and narrow the road that leads to life, and only a few find it."* (Matthew 7:13–14 NIV) We might entertain the possibility that the **wide gate** and the **broad road** are the path of FEAR. If so, that means fear leads to destruction. Then we would have to consider that the **small gate** and the **narrow road** is FAITH in Jesus the Messiah. Faith in Jesus leads to life.

Let's Talk or Think About It

- **Is my life built on fear or on faith in Jesus?"**

- **FEAR has a god and its name is Mammon. Based on what we learned about Mammon, how would you help someone know whether they are following Mammon or God in a decision? What does the following of Mammon look like?**

- **FAITH has a God and His name is Jesus. Personally pick or have the group pick a significant decision that is coming up and talk about what Mammon and what Jesus would look like in the decision. Would this make a difference in the way you make the decision?**

[This might work well with a significant financial decision]

- **Why is entering through Jesus and walking the narrow path so important? Base your answer on Matthew 7:13-14**

CHAPTER 12

"The Crossing"

In our journey out of bondage, many different processes occur, several of which we have discussed in previous chapters. These events happen as we are redeemed from our slave master, Satan, and begin to follow our redeemer, Jesus. Although this process can be time consuming and extremely challenging, we have a powerful and comforting promise from the Lord as recorded in the book of Romans.

> *And we know that all things work together for good to those who love God, to those who are the called according to His purpose. 29 For whom He foreknew, He also predestined to be conformed to the image of His Son, that He might be the firstborn among many brethren.* (Romans 8:28–29 NKJV)

As awesome as it is to be redeemed from slavery and bondage, and as amazing as it is to walk through the journey of learning to know and obey the voice of the Lord, there comes a time that moving out is required. Without a doubt, I would say every one of us wants to live in the land of God's abundance, but there are real challenges with that journey. When the Israelites faced those challenges, it caused them to shrink back in fear.

There were three main hindrances that caused the Israelites to question moving into the abundant life God had promised.

First Hindrance: The Jordan River

The first of the three major hindrances we will face when crossing into the promised abundant plan of God is the "Jordan River experience." After 40 years, Israel was finally ready to obey the Lord and to enter the Promised Land. Yet, there was a serious obstacle in their way. They had to take the entire population of Israel over a flooded Jordan River.

For the most part, Israel's journey out of bondage had been across the desert. Now they faced a different challenge. Once again, the Israelites were staring at a huge hindrance threatening their ability to move into abundance. At this point, the Lord gave Joshua instructions about how to cross the Jordan.

Read Joshua 3:11–13 and 3:17

What are the lessons we need to learn from Israel when it comes to entering in?

There are some very important principles found within this instruction to Israel that may be of significant help to all who wish to move into the abundance of the Lord. To move across the Jordan, a few things need to happen.

First, the Covenant of the Lord must lead you. The covenant was the "Ark of the Covenant," which represented the Word, the Presence, and the Power of God. For Christ followers today, these three things must be placed in front of us as the priority of our lives and as the source of our truth. Today, these are represented in a variety of ways.

For example, knowing and obeying the Word of the Lord instead of our human senses requires faith. As we follow God's Word, His Holy Spirit will also lead us into all truth. Being filled with God's Spirit comes by being born again and then walking daily in a state of being filled.

Second, the Leaders of the family must lead the way. If you will remember 40 years earlier as Israel considered going into the Promised Land, the majority of the original 12 leaders said, *"No, we will not go in."* This stopped the entire nation from obeying the Lord and caused them to suffer for 40 years. God decided that twelve new leaders must lead the way into the Promised Land.

So, if you are a leader in your family, your church, your community, or your nation, it is vital that you have faith in God's Word and courage to lead the way.

Third, the step of faith into your "Jordan" stops its power. The Jordan River represents the place where our position of "self-god" is put off and full surrender to the Lord is accomplished. Now notice what happens to the power of the old life when you take the first step of faith into your Jordan. The flow of power is <u>shut off</u>!

Think about it. When you finally take that action of faith, the power that has hindered you all of your life is shut off, and you will be able to move ahead into God's promise. That is extremely exciting to me! But, let me show you something else that just might give you even more motivation to walk into your Jordan. When you step in by faith, the power that hindered you will also be shut off downstream. That means that the power of sin and hindrance will not be able to hurt and hinder your children, and your grandchildren!

Two types of "Jordans" we may face as we learn to live in God's abundance.

1.   *The Jordan of a Remaining Deception*

As we remain the god of our own lives, we have no power to overcome the controlling deceptions that remain hooked in our souls. These controlling deceptions come in thousands of different forms. One potential deception that may be controlling us is that a sinful temptation is the identifying label of our life. Maybe we struggle with homosexual temptations, but it does not mean that we are identified as a homosexual. It means we are a born-again Christ follower that wrestles against a controlling deception that is designed to kill, steal, and destroy. But as soon as we surrender to the Lordship of Jesus, the power of the controlling deception is shut off. It is with the power of Jesus in our life and the Word of God as the agent that transforms our minds that we can now walk in the freedom that the Lord provides.

2. *The Jordan of a Remaining Bondage*

There are numerous things that can remain as bondage to us even after we give our lives to follow Jesus. These are the things that found their way in when we were living in bondage and still remain hooked to our souls. I see a lot of giant bondages in churches today. Some examples include fear and addictions such as drugs, alcohol, and pornography. Another area of bondage is blindness to the reality of how sin controls us and hurts those around us. A bondage of unwillingness to submit to the Word of the Lord and the leadership of His Spirit.

When we face these bondages, which act as a Jordan River of hindrance, then the Lord will instruct us how to step into that river with faith. Seeing and acknowledging that bondage, gives the Lord a chance to let us regain that territory that had been controlled by the power of sin in our life. Each step into the river will give back more and more that had been stolen from our ability to walk in freedom.

What is YOUR personal Jordan River (hindrance) that keeps you from being able to enter into God's abundance for your life?

What principles or promises of Scripture can you find in which God provides Truths that counteract the Lies that hinder you?

Second Hindrance: The Presence of Giants

The second of the three main enemies that caused the Israelites to question moving into the abundant life God had promised was the giants.

This is a very interesting subject that Scripture introduces us to. As I will show you, the Bible talks about a race of people who were truly of giant size. The Bible uses several different names to identify these large people. They are at times called Nephilim, Rephaites, or Anak. The size of these giants is amazing in itself, but scriptural history reveals that these giants were a strange combination of human women and "sons of God."

Before this gets too weird for you, let me show you one of these scriptures. Giants were first mentioned in Genesis.

> *Now a population explosion took place upon the earth. It was at this time that beings from the spirit world[s] looked upon the beautiful earth women and took any they desired to be their wives. Then Jehovah said, "My Spirit must not forever be disgraced in man, wholly evil as he is. I will give him 120 years to mend his ways."*
>
> *In those days, and even afterwards, when the evil beings from the spirit world were sexually involved with human women, their children became giants, of whom so many legends are told. (*Genesis 6:1–4 Living Bible)

Whatever the origin of these giants, they were real and were intimidating to God's people as they were entering the Land of Promise.

Possible GIANTS we may face as we learn to live in God's abundance.

The Giant of a Secularized Government

It is my opinion that with the elections of 2012, the Christian-based, conservative portion of America, for the first time in our 200-year history, became the minority. With this new reality, the liberal majority of our country appears to have the power to institutionalize their anti-Biblical morals and anti-Christian positions. As this occurs, more and more of the principles of Scripture will be removed from the public square, and our culture will be pushed more toward secular socialism with an overlord known as the centralized government. As this controlling, destructive spirit increases, the reality of life in America as our forefathers saw and the freedoms of Christ followers will begin to lessen. I predict that within a few short years, Christians will be labeled as threats to the government, and persecution will increase as the liberal media and ungodly government officials fully integrate to accomplish this dark vision.

If this is the future of Christ followers, then living in God's abundance requires facing the threat of the giant known as "a godless government." The question is, will Christ followers have the courage, perseverance, and faith to live in God's abundance in the face of what will likely become a one-world government that will usher in the Anti-Christ as foretold in Scripture? Our unshakeable position will be our faith in the work and message of Jesus the Messiah.

The Giant of Americanized Christianity

Many churches and Christian organizations seek to appeal to the progressively secular population. The giant of Americanized Christianity attempts to tame God and His scriptural demands so that we can create a personalized Christianity in our own image. The best way I can describe this giant is to compare it to the philosophy of the huge discount conglomerate known as Wal-Mart. This Americanized Christianity is a type of Wal-Mart religion. It makes the church socially acceptable by making it low in demands, time requirements, cost, and hassle. This type of church becomes more focused on pleasing ME and my wants rather than on God and His plan for our lives. The size and popularity of this form of religion will be a giant to those who hear the call to lay their **me-focused** lives down so that Jesus and God's Word become our master. This alone allows for abundant living in a decaying society.

The Giant of the End Times

The third Giant of our day may well be the fall of the world's economic system that will usher in the end times, a one-world government, and the rise of the anti-Christ. As this occurs, II Timothy reveals the social conditions that will develop.

> *But understand this, that in the last days there will come times of difficulty. For people will be lovers of self, lovers of money, proud, arrogant, abusive, disobedient to their parents, ungrateful, unholy, heartless, unappeasable, slanderous, without self-control, brutal, not loving good, treacherous, reckless, swollen with conceit, lovers of pleasure rather than lovers of God, having the appearance of godliness, but denying its power. Avoid such people.* (II Timothy 3:1–5 ESV)

It is within this type of social pressure that Christ followers will need to walk closely with the Lord, know His voice, and have great courage to walk in obedience to Him. Even in this social degeneration, true Christ followers will walk in the abundance of the Lord.

Go back and scan the possible Giants that we may face in our day as we seek to walk in the abundance of the Lord.

Consider how you will respond based on God's Word if you face one of these:

- **Secularized Government**
- **Me-Focused Church Environment**
- **Failing Economic System**
- **Any other Giants you see us facing**

We've talked about the Jordan River and facing giants as being hindrances for finding the abundant life God has promised. Let's examine the third hindrance.

Third Hindrance: Fortified Cities

The third major enemy we may face when crossing into the Promised Land is the walled cities. One of the hindrances listed by ten of the twelve spies who were sent in to investigate the Land of Promise was that the cities of the land were fortified and very large. It was because of this hindrance that the majority report of the spies came back negative: "We cannot go into the land that God promised us."

The first city that Israel faced was Jericho. Cities like Jericho are large hindrances that a Christ-follower faces that say, "You cannot go any further. This is the limit of your freedom. We are too big, too strong, too intimidating for you to ever have a chance to find victory." Their demand is for us to be intimidated. The sheer size of the obstacle seems to demand that we not even try to move into abundance.

Here are a few fortified cities we may face as we learn to live in God's abundance.

The City of Demonic Strongholds

These are demonic strongholds that still have their hooks in our soul. We discussed the power of these in Chapter 3. Strongholds are always based on a lie. Mental strongholds have to be defeated by identifying them, confessing them, and then repenting of them. We then receive spiritual healing from the Lord by transforming our mind through God's Word. This is the truth that removes the lie. Strongholds may manifest in our life through continued addiction, depression, overwhelming fear, a spirit of poverty, or thousands of other tactics that the demonic uses to stop us from entering into the abundant life.

The City of Legalism

We may face disapproval and rejection by those who are religious and hold to strict legalism, or the letter of the law. Grace and freedom of the Lord fly in the face of those who are attempting to earn their way into heaven by being religious and good. We may find this rejection brought by even our closest family members or friends. As painful as rejection is, the freedom of the Lord and the abundance of His life for us are well worth the price of rejection we may experience.

The City of Tolerance

In our society, we constantly face the increasing social pressure to reject Jesus as the Savior of the world and to recreate Him as a narrow-minded, legalistic bigot. The new social pressure will be the insistence that all forms of religion lead to God. To fit in with our increasing secular culture, "tolerance" is elevated as the highest form of spirituality, and Christianity is belittled as a crutch for the weak minded.

I would like for you to notice one important truth revealed about the walled cities we will be facing. It is found in Scripture where it says, *"Now Jericho [the first limitation] was tightly shut up because of the Israelites."* (Joshua 6:1 NIV)

Why was the hindrance of Jericho tightly shut up? People were terrified of the God of the people of Israel.

Please write this truth deeply into your heart:

> **Although the hindrances we face look huge and intimidating, the truth is that the enemies of God are terrified of Him and of His people.**

There are great benefits before us as we cross over the Jordan and begin to live in God's abundance. But, as we have seen, there are real, scary obstacles that we will face as we learn to live in God's abundance. Each one is already defeated, however, as we learn to walk by faith in God's Word and trust the leading of the Holy Spirit in our lives.

Let's go on across our Jordan and enjoy the freedoms and abundance of the Lord!

> *Then Caleb silenced the people before Moses and said, "We should go up and take possession of the land, for we can certainly do it."* (Numbers 13:30 NIV)

Let's Talk or Think About It

- Are you currently facing a hindrance like a Fortified City?

- What are you experiencing?

- What Scripture can you find that teaches you how to defeat these?

    Demonic Strongholds

    Disapproval and Rejection

    Increasing Societal Rejection of Jesus

- As you read in Joshua 3–5, what Scriptures do you find that will assist you as you proceed into the promise God has for you?

SECTION #4

In Abundance

CHAPTER 13

"Hearing, Knowing, and Following God's Voice"

The spiritual skill of hearing when God speaks—knowing what He is saying and having the courage to follow His instructions completely—is the most important skill for the true Christ follower to obtain. Hearing God will be especially important in a time when the church is seen as obsolete and as greater tribulation occurs. It is during this time that deceiving spirits will increase and Satan's deception will be unmatched by anyone or anything. His ability to deceive is clearly defined in the gospel of John. *"He was a murderer from the beginning, not holding to the truth, for there is no truth in him. When he lies, he speaks his native language, for he is a liar and the father of lies."* (John 8:44 NIV)

Have you ever had an experience in which you knew you were hearing the voice of the Lord?

What was it like?

What did He tell you?

How do you know it was from Him?

And Jesus answered them, "See that no one leads you astray. 5 For many will come in my name, saying, 'I am the Christ,' and they will lead many astray."(Matthew 24:4–5 ESV)

Then He said just a few verses later, *"For false christs and false prophets will appear and perform great signs and miracles to deceive even the elect—if that were possible."* (Matthew 24:24 NIV)

If we know God's plan is for His people to walk in His abundance—even though there will be hindrances, obstacles, dangers, and deceptions—we must also understand and develop one spiritual skill: knowing and following God's voice.

Have you had an experience where you heard from the Lord but did not obey?

What kept you from taking action on what He told you?

Four Different Soils

To develop this skill, we must understand that people hear the word of the Lord in different ways. In Matthew 13, Mark 4, and Luke 8, we can study the Word of Jesus as He was teaching on this very subject. I will place the Matthew passage here for your convenience, but I recommend that you also read the passages in Mark and Luke before moving on.

Read Matthew 13:3–23

Jesus often spoke through an earthly story with a spiritual application. In this parable, there was a farmer who went out to sow seed that would produce his desired crop. "Seed" in this story represents the truth of God as found in His Word. But, on this farmer's land there were four different types of soil that represent different kinds of people. It is the soil types that Jesus uses to help us understand the four different ways people receive God's Word.

Hard Soil

The first type of person is one who hears about God or even hears from Him, but will not accept the message. Because they won't accept the message, they don't believe. Belief is very important in hearing what God is saying, but this person does not believe. Therefore, the Word (or the seed) that was given to him is snatched away and has no impact on his life.

Rocky Soil

The second type of person is one who hears a message about God's Kingdom and loves it. Scripture says they receive it with joy. But, when a time of difficulty or testing comes along, they fall away and begin to doubt the Word.

Perseverance is the ability to remain, even when the going gets tough, even when questions seem to have no answers. The rocky soil is where many American "Christians" seem to live. They are easily offended, flighty, and uncommitted—bouncing around from one church to another in their search to find a place that makes them happy.

But, as soon as challenge comes, they are off on their search again. They represent a seed never still enough to bear fruit. Bishop T. D. Jakes says pastors are failing all over the nation as they try to plant good seed in rocky soil lives that have no root. With no root there will never be any fruit.

Thorny Soil

The third type of person is one who hears the Word and receives the seed with the full intention of being a Christ follower. But, the influence of the world is more appealing, or at least more demanding. Due to entertainment, money, relationships, or fear for survival, they have no room for seeds to develop and grow. The seed is choked out by the things of the world, which the parable calls "weeds." This person never matures; therefore, they never find God's will and fulfill His purpose.

Good Soil

The fourth type of person is one who hears the Word and understands it. This means he hears the message of the Gospel, which states that Jesus loves us. It goes on to say we are broken and dead in our spirit because of our sin condition. It also tells us Jesus died on the cross to pay for our forgiveness and He, through the Holy Spirit, will come into our life and take up residence. The Good News is that He will be the forgiver, teacher, leader, spiritual-gift giver, and master of our lives. The good-soil person accepts the Word and, because of faith, retains it and perseveres in it to produce a fruitful, spiritual crop throughout life.

The hard truth about this parable is that if we are any type of soil other than Good Soil, we will not remain and will not make it into the life of God's abundance in the area where His seed is planted.

In order to develop "good soil" or the ability to receive the Word of God into our life so that it can produce a healthy life that comes from the Lord's Kingdom, there is a story in scripture that will give us a model for our life. There is an interesting observation in the book of Acts about the Bereans. As you read this verse, what sticks out to you that makes the Bereans more noble?

> *"Now these were more noble than those in Thessalonica, in that they received the word with all readiness of the mind, examining the Scriptures daily, whether these things were so."* (Acts 17:11 NAS)

What could YOU do that would make you more like the Bereans?

Let's look at a couple of subjects that each of us face in our daily life. We will look at these through biblical instructions and then compare how each type of "soil" responds to the "seed" of biblical truth.

The Seed of Biblical Finances

Let's take a look at a topic familiar to all of us, one we all deal with at times: money. As we dive into this issue, we will consider the four soil types and how they correspond to the spiritual seed principle of money.

Let's begin with a Word from God found in Malachi:

> *"Will a man rob God? Yet you rob Me [God speaking].*
>
> *"But you ask, 'How do we rob You?' In tithes and offerings. You are under a curse—the whole nation of you—because you are robbing Me. Bring the whole tithe [first 10% of your income] into the storehouse [the church], that there may be food in My house.*
>
> *Can a person rob God? You indeed are robbing me, but you say, 'How are we robbing you?' In tithes and contributions! You are bound for judgment because you are robbing me—this whole nation is guilty.*
>
> *"Bring the entire tithe into the storehouse so that there may be food in my temple. Test me in this matter," says the Lord who rules over all, "to see if I will not open for you the windows of heaven and pour out for you a blessing until there is no room for it all. Then I will stop the plague from ruining your crops, and the vine will not lose its fruit before harvest," says the Lord who rules over all. All nations will call you happy, for you indeed will live in a delightful land," says the Lord who rules over all.*(Malachi 3:8–12 NET)

Records of churches in America show that only about 25% of the people who attend church practice this biblical seed principle. In other words, 75% of church attenders in America are soils that never produce fruit. This could be one reason America is now a post-Christian nation.

How would the following SOILS deal with this SEED from God's Word?

The Hard Soil

These people hear the Word of the Lord as a manipulation from the preacher, attempting to get more money out of their pocket. Because of their initial mistrust, they simply do not believe this Word. Because they do not believe, there is no faith to receive the seed, and they walk away with no intention to ever give what they perceive to be theirs to a church. These people lose any of the promised blessings they could have enjoyed if they believed.

The Rocky Soil

These people hear the Word of the Lord about tithing and like the sound of the promised blessings. They might actually begin to give the next Sunday, but then the next week some unexpected bills come in and they begin to think, "Where are my open window blessings from God?" So they quickly stop giving. There will be no fruit produced from this person because they didn't believe enough to remain faithful to God's Word when the situation got a little tough.

The Thorny Soil

These people hear the Word of the Lord and have enough faith to start giving for a significant season. At the end of the first quarter, however, they totaled up the amount they have given and start thinking about all of the material items they could have purchased with that money. Thoughts begin to surface like, "We could have gone to Florida on that money. We could have bought that ski boat. We could have really built up our retirement account. We could have paid off that debt we have." Before long, they have convinced themselves that material possessions are more important than living in God's abundance.

The Good Soil

These people hear the Word of the Lord and believe it despite every doubt or worldly use of this money. They tenaciously begin to follow the Word of God and give 10% of all that God blesses them with each week.

Even when tested by surprise bills, they do not back down because they have decided to trust God's Word when they are facing financing trials. They believe God's promise: *"Test Me in this and see if I will not throw open the windows of heaven and pour out so much blessing that you will not have enough room for it."* (Malachi 3:10 NIV) The person whose heart is good soil remains faithful over days, weeks, months, years, and even decades.

Because of their perseverance, they now openly tell others of the hundreds of ways the Lord has blessed them as they live in His abundance. They not only obeyed in the tithe, but also learned a principle that makes God's abundance even more productive. II Corinthians 9:6–15 tells us how to produce an even more abundant harvest in God's land of promised blessing.

> *"My point is this: The person who sows sparingly will also reap sparingly, and the person who sows generously will also reap generously. Each one of you should give just as he has decided in his heart, not reluctantly or under compulsion, because God loves a cheerful giver. And God is able to make all grace overflow to you so that because you have enough of everything in every way at all times, you will overflow in every good work. Just as it is written, "He has scattered widely, he has given to the poor; his righteousness remains forever." Now God who provides seed for the sower and bread for food will provide and multiply your supply of seed and will cause the harvest of your righteousness to grow. You will be enriched in every way so that you may be generous on every occasion, which is producing through us thanksgiving to God, because the service of this ministry is not only providing for the needs of the saints but is also overflowing with many thanks to God. Through the evidence of this service they will glorify God because of your obedience to your confession in the gospel of Christ and the generosity of your sharing with them and with everyone. And in their prayers on your behalf they long for you because of the extraordinary grace God has*

> *shown to you. Thanks be to God for his indescribable gift!"*
> (II Corinthians 9:6-15 NET)

What were your thoughts about the tithe and the different responses?

The Seed of Biblical Marriages

Another area that we can apply the different soil types is in the biblical principles of marriage.

> *"Wives, be subject to your husbands as you are to the Lord. 23 For the husband is the head of the wife just as Christ is the head of the church, the body of which he is the Savior. 24 Just as the church is subject to Christ, so also wives ought to be, in everything, to their husbands.*
>
> *Husbands, love your wives, just as Christ loved the church and gave himself up for her, in order to make her holy by cleansing her with the washing of water by the word, so as to present the church to himself in splendor, without a spot or wrinkle or anything of the kind—yes, so that she may be holy and without blemish."* (Ephesians 5:22–27 NRSV)

The Hard Soil Wife and Husband

This couple may hear the scriptural counsel for a successful marriage relationship, but they are so enmeshed in the media's portrayal of sex-based relationships that they consider biblical insights as nothing more than archaic and restrictive rules. In their minds, these prudish rules have no impact on their socially enlightened life. The wife hears the word "submit" and immediately says, "This will never happen!" Then the husband hears the words, "and gave himself up for her," and in his mind he says, "I will never give myself up for her; that is simply out of the question." Therefore, the principles for successful relationships have no place in their lives.

The Rocky Soil Wife and Husband

This couple comes to church to find some help for their *less than perfect* marriage. When the husband hears that the "wife is to submit to the husband in everything," he gets really excited with all of the possibilities. And when the wife hears that the husband is to "give himself up for her," she gets giddy with excitement. Then, when the instruction puts expectations on them personally, they only want the benefits that come from the Godly spouse, but have no willingness to fulfill their role for healthy relationships. At this point, the truths heard simply cannot take root because their soil is hardened.

The Thorny Soil Wife and Husband

This couple comes to hear the Pastor teach on successful marriages. They even set up some counseling times to try to give room for the seeds of God's Word to be planted in their life. But, with the busyness of work, house responsibilities, children's activities, recreation, and a new multimedia system, they simply do not have time to apply and practice the principles they have learned. The seed of God's Word is choked out by activities and material possessions.

The Good Soil Wife and Husband

This couple hears of the personal responsibilities associated with a Godly marriage. They understand that the instruction simply says each partner will need to take a secondary place to one another. The wife hears and practices submission in a way done for the Lord. She understands that God has built into the husband a deep-seated need for honor. This honor is shown to him in hundreds of ways, but each way starts with the submission of his wife. The husband sees that the greatest love he can show his wife is by putting her first. When he does, the wife is given a safe environment in which she can flourish. This "good soil" couple hears the words of life from Scripture and takes them to heart so they have room to produce good fruit. This marriage will prosper as long as the Lord gives them life.

What were your thoughts about the issue of husband and wife responsibilities?

How to Hear God's Voice

We have looked at a couple of illustrations about how people hear and respond to the Word of the Lord. Now let's take some time to find how God speaks to us and what we need to add to our own hearts to become "good soil."

Because of our awareness of a growing spiritual deception that is coming, it is vital that we use God's Word in Scripture as our foundation for how we will learn to listen to God. Let's look at how others have heard from God throughout Scripture.

God Speaks Through Reading His Word

Israel's King David wrote this Psalm about basing his life on the truths and principles of God's Word. If we would personalize this section of Scripture, perhaps we would be able to hear God's voice.

Read Psalm 119:97–105

God speaks in a number of different ways, as we are getting ready to learn. But, all of the following ways must be measured against God's Word as revealed in Scripture. This is the only absolute way to build a guard against deception.

God Speaks Through Prayer

We are often taught that prayer happens when we bring our "wish list" to the Lord, treating Him as the big Santa Clause in the sky. In actuality, God is our Creator and He desires that we have a real relationship with Him daily. One of the best ways for this to happen is to set aside time each day to get into a private place and spend time with the Lord. We take time to read and meditate on His Word. We ask Him to speak to us by revealing new truths each day. We write down what He shows us in a spiritual journal. By doing these things, we begin to transform our minds from demonic lies to the truths of God's Kingdom. The transition happens when we stop telling Him everything we want and our prayers become more like, "What do you want to say to me today, Lord? What truth do you want me to build my life on? What do I need to know today, Lord, to help me hear Your voice and walk in Your abundance?"

God Speaks Through People

I believe it is vitally important that we develop a strong spiritual support system in our life. God's plan is His church. He will sometimes speak to us clearly through our spiritual family. Your Pastor spends hours each week listening to the Lord and studying Scripture so that he can bring a living word that will help to build up your spiritual muscles. But your pastor is not the only person that God will use to speak His message to us. Within the church, there are spiritual gifts given by the Lord to His people: gifts such as prophecy, teaching, encouraging, leadership, mercy, wisdom, knowledge, healing, and many more. As you engage in your church, God will at times speak through others by the gift He has given them, and you will know it is His Word.

God Speaks Through His Creation

The Apostle Paul wrote these words that show us how God speaks even through the things He has created.

Read Romans 1:18–20

The simple truth is that the magnificent creation of God—planets, earth, humanity, the universe, and everything in it—speaks to the fact that there must be a creator. And as the Bible starts with these words, we know that our God **IS** the Creator: "IN THE BEGINNING GOD..." (Genesis 1:1 NIV) As we take in God's creation, it will often testify to God's amazing greatness.

God Speaks Through His Holy Spirit

When we take the leap of faith and trust the good news of Jesus by receiving Him into our life as our forgiver and our leader, He places His Holy Spirit inside us. Here are some things scripture reveals about the work of the Holy Spirit within us:

He speaks to our spirit: *"However, you are not in the flesh but in the Spirit, if indeed the Spirit of God dwells in you. But if anyone does not have the Spirit of Christ, he does not belong to Him."* (Rom. 8:9 NIV)

He speaks in the believer's mind: *"That is the Spirit of truth, whom the world cannot receive, because it does not behold Him or know Him, but you know Him because He abides with you, and will be in you."* (John 14:17 NIV)

He speaks in ways to give us life: *"But if the Spirit of Him who raised Jesus from the dead dwells in you, He who raised Christ Jesus from the dead will also give life to your mortal bodies through His Spirit who indwells you."* (Rom. 8:11 NIV)

He speaks to confirm truth: *"And it is the Spirit who bears witness, because the Spirit is the truth."* (1 John 5:6 NIV)

God Speaks Through Visions and Dreams

In the New Testament, the Apostle Peter quoted the prophet Joel when he wrote these words, *"'In the last days,' God says, 'I will pour out my Spirit on all people. Your sons and daughters will prophesy, your young men will see visions, your old men will dream dreams.'"* (Acts 2:17 NIV) Let's be clear and careful here. Not every dream we have at night is from God, and not all visions are from God. All forms of communication we believe are from God are to be tested by Scripture. If the dream or vision contradicts a word, principle, or truth of Scripture it is to be discarded.

As we come to the end of this chapter, let me encourage you to become a true Christ follower by learning to hear, recognize, and understand the voice of the Lord in your life. It will take some time and effort because we have been trained to listen to the voice of our old slave masters, the desires of our flesh, and the loud messages of our world.

But Jesus said, *"My sheep listen to my voice; I know them and they follow Me."* (John 10:27 NIV) Let us adhere to this truth spoken by Jesus Himself and learn to tune our spiritual ears to His voice.

Let's Talk or Think About It

- Above are some suggestions about how God may speak to those who want to hear His communications. Which method or methods does God most often use to speak to you?

- Why do you think knowing God's Word is important in our day?

- Why do you think knowing God's Word is important in our day?

- The Old Testament book of Deuteronomy contains a challenge for Jewish families. It is called the "SHEMA YISRAEL." Read Deuteronomy 6:4-9

- Why do you think this was a central prayer in Jewish families?

- What truths do you find in this passage?

CHAPTER 14

"Living In God's Promise"

As I was writing the closing chapter of this book, an event happened that caused my view to expand a bit more about living in God's Promised Land.

Yesterday, my father-in-law passed away after a several-year battle with Parkinson's disease. This was the same disease that brought my father to his death just a year and a half earlier. This expanded my vision because this earth in its fallen condition is not our final home. It is damaged and broken because of sin and the chaos created by the demonic.

As Christ followers, however, we are to be ambassadors of the Lord's Kingdom while we live in this world that is foreign to us. We are to share His message of hope, healing, and salvation with all in which we come in contact. We are to be a light that will help some find Jesus. But, this same light in us will repel others because they love the darkness of their sin rather than light. The bottom line is we are to be ambassadors for Jesus. Any person who does not know the salvation and transformation of the Lord Jesus lives this life in vain, is trapped by bondages, and will face an eternity in a place designed for the punishment of Satan and his demons. Scripture calls it, Hell.

The other side is the good news for Christians. Redeemed people have not only the hope of heaven, which is the true Promised Land, but also the confidence of living in and for God's Kingdom even on this earth. Jesus taught us to pray this way through the model prayer in Matthew: *"Our*

Father in heaven, hallowed be Your name, Your kingdom come, Your will be done, on earth as it is in heaven." (Matthew 6:9–10 NIV)

We are to live a life of worship toward God and also to pray for His kingdom will to be done here on earth just like it is in heaven. Heaven is the ultimate Promised Land, but I also believe that truly born-again Christ followers enjoy the blessings of God's promises right here on this broken earth. If this is the case, then what does the abundant life in Christ look like? I would like to propose that there are approximately seven segments of life that, when lived under the Lordship of Jesus and in unison with the truth of Scripture, allow us to live in the Lord's abundance. Here are seven life segments I see:

1. A Born-Again Spirit

To live in God's abundance, a person has to understand the journey from bondage to abundance and receive Jesus as their personal Lord (Master) and Savior (Forgiver). They have to walk through the Romans Road of scriptures and give their lives to Jesus.

Consider walking through these scriptures to check your own spiritual condition and to be able to share with others. Mark these in your Bible as you go.

> *"For all have sinned and fall short of the glory of God."* (Romans 3:23 NIV)

This is a clear statement about the fallen condition of all human beings. In our natural state, we are separated from God because of a sin condition.

> *"But God demonstrates His own love for us in this: While we were still sinners, Christ died for us."* (Romans 5:8 NIV)

This is where the Good News begins. This is where hope is returned to the human condition. This is where God provides a full payment for our sin debt.

> *"For the wages of sin is death, but the gift of God is eternal life in Christ Jesus our Lord."* (Romans 6:23 NIV)

The original condition of man is that he is lost in sin. This means that the spirit of man is dead because of sin. Anyone who dies with this death in their spirit faces an eternity separated from God. Scripture calls this the "second death." But, God has provided a gift to everyone who comes to Jesus and agrees that their sin has separated them from God, then repents or turns from sin to Jesus and by faith receives the gift of forgiveness. God promises eternal life in Christ Jesus.

> *"God made Him who had no sin [Jesus] to be sin for us, so that in Him we might become the righteousness of God."* (II Corinthians 5:21 NIV)

This is how the transaction happens. God put all of the sin of all humanity on Jesus at the cross. When Jesus died there, He paid the sin debt for all humanity. But, only those who come by faith to Jesus receive this gift.

> *"The word is near you; it is in your mouth and in your heart, that is, the word of faith we are proclaiming: That if you confess with your mouth, "Jesus is Lord," and believe in your heart that God raised Him from the dead, you will be saved. For it is with your heart that you believe and are justified, and it is with your mouth that you confess and are saved."* (Romans 10:8–10 NIV)

Two steps are given here that define the salvation transaction. First, there is BELIEF or faith. If you believe or have faith that Jesus died on the cross, then you have the ability to receive that forgiveness by faith. The second step is CONFESSION. Confession is sharing with the people of your life that you have become a Christ follower.

> *"Everyone who calls on the name of the Lord will be saved."* (Romans 10:13 NIV)

Now we can see why sharing this good news with everyone we influence is so important. IF they will receive this news and come to Jesus, they too can be saved.

2. A Transformed Soul

To live in God's abundance, we must understand Paul's theology, which states that man is created in the image of God. The three-part nature of our soul is made up of our mind, will, and emotions.

Mind: What We Think

Read Romans 12:2

Our minds have been trained since birth to learn to live on planet Earth. This Earth is also the abode of the demonic, and much of what we have learned is based on the deceptions and fears of Satan's plan. That is why Scripture says, *"Do not be conformed any longer to the pattern of this world."* Then Paul says that to be transformed, we must also renew our minds. This process begins with salvation, but is accomplished by replacing demonic lies and fears with God's Word, which is truth, and His love, which casts out all fear.

Will: What We Choose

Have we made God's Word, its promises, and its principles the faith positions for our life? It is from God's Word that ideas are formed in our minds. From these Godly ideas come belief. From belief comes action. So as the Word is engrafted into our minds, our choices become guided by the Spirit of Truth and will lead to abundant life. Jesus tells us, *"The thief [Satan] comes only to steal and kill and destroy; I have come that they may have life, and have it to the full."* (John 10:10 NIV)

What do you believe the Lord meant when He said, "The thief comes only to steal and kill and destroy; I have come that they might have life, and have it to the full."

Emotions: What We Feel

Our feelings are simply responses to our minds and choices. Feelings lead us poorly. All they know how to do is follow our godly or ungodly choices. Therefore, if God's Word is transforming our mind and our choices are based on its truth and principles, then our emotions will be of love, joy, peace, patience, kindness, goodness, faithfulness, gentleness, and self-control. (Galatians 5:22–23 NIV) We must be aware that our emotions can be misguided because of sin. It will take a little time for these emotional responders to be healed and to function properly, but be encouraged in that our emotions will be healed and transformed as we follow the Lord.

3.   A Spirit-Empowered Life

To live in God's abundance, we must understand the design of the Jewish Tabernacle. It was made up of three parts: the outer court, the Holy Place, and the Holy of Holies. Similarly, we are made up of three parts.

The outer court corresponds to our physical bodies, which are temporary. The Holy Place corresponds to our eternal souls. The Holy of Holies corresponds to our spirits, which are also eternal. John 3:6 says, *"Flesh gives birth to flesh, but the **Spirit** [Holy Spirit] gives birth to **spirit** [man's spirit that is dead in trespass and sin]."* The spirit of mankind, when redeemed by Jesus, is cleansed of all of its sin. Once cleansed, the Holy Spirit comes to live inside our spirit to become our leader.

As the Spirit of God comes to live within us, He brings gifts for us to use within the body of Christ. Read more about gifts of the Holy Spirit in Romans 12:3–8 and I Corinthians 12:7–11.

4.   Clear Life Mission

To live in God's abundance, we must understand our God-given purpose through knowledge of our mission. Without a purpose, life simply becomes existence or survival until death. But, with a God-given mission, every day is an opportunity to fulfill the purposes God placed in our hearts.

This is my personal mission:

> *To represent God's Kingdom Will in all relationships and situations.*

You will need to determine YOUR own mission based on how God has designed you and the burden that He has placed in your heart. Your mission will be different. Whatever your mission is, it needs to be able to apply anywhere. Begin to ask God why He made you and what His mission is for your life. Begin to pay attention to the needs around you that burden you and pay attention to the passion God has placed in your heart.

What makes you tick? What gets you excited? What makes you want to jump in and do something? Chances are this is part of the mission God has planned in your life.

5. God-Based Relationships

To live in God's abundance, it is vital that we live in God's plan for all relationships.

Abundant Marriage or Successful Singleness

God, in His sovereign design, chooses some to be single. Sometimes this call is for their entire life and sometimes only for a season. For some, this calling comes with a lot of angst as they long for love, romance, family, friendship, and partnership. For others, the call to singleness seems easy and preferable for their life. People who find themselves single can find their fulfillment in their relationship with the Lord and use their freedom to advance the missions He has placed in their hearts.

I cannot actually pretend to understand the challenges and heartaches of singleness, especially for those who long for marriage. But, I do know that God is good, He is all knowing, and He is all powerful. With this, I must trust that His plan is best for my life, even when I don't understand or agree.

The Apostle Paul explained it like this:

Read I Corinthians 7:25–31

For those God has chosen for marriage, the Apostle Paul gives the following instructions:

> **Wives**, *submit to your husbands as unto the Lord. For the husband is the head of the wife as Christ is head of the church, His body, of which He is the Savior. Now as the church submits to Christ, so also wives should submit to their husbands in everything.* (Ephesians 5:22–24 NRSV)

Notice the HUGE CHALLENGE for the wife: that she is to "submit to her husband."

> **Husbands**, *love your wives, just as Christ loved the church and gave himself up for her, in order to make her holy by cleansing her with the washing of water by the word, so as to present the church to himself in splendor, without a spot or wrinkle or anything of the kind—yes, so that she may be holy and without blemish. In the same way, husbands should love their wives as they do their own bodies. He who loves his wife loves himself.* (Ephesians 5:25–28 NRSV)

Notice the HUGE CHALLENGE for the husband: "he is to give himself up for her." For a marriage relationship to work, each partner must be willing to lay down his or her selfishness for the benefit of the other. It takes the denial of self in order for this blessed marriage be to accomplished. As you can see, marriage is very difficult, but God uses its challenges to shape us into the image of His Son, Jesus.

Blessed Children

Children are a great blessing. If the Lord chooses to bless you with children, keep them as a high priority in your life's work and ministry. The time you spend with them is the best time spent in your life. Remember, we only get to hold them for a moment, so love them, protect them, train them up in the Lord.

> *"Don't you see that children are God's best gift? The fruit of the womb his generous legacy? Like a warrior's fistful of arrows are the children of a vigorous youth. Oh, how blessed are you parents, with your quivers full of children! Your enemies don't stand a chance against you; you'll sweep them right off your doorstep."* (Psalm 127:3–5 The Message)

> *"Train a child in the way he should go, and when he is old he will not turn from it."* (Proverbs 22:6 NIV)

Immediate and Extended Family

Our first and most important ministry or business is our family. Love them unconditionally. Let the Spirit of Jesus flow as blessings from your life into your family. Serve them as Jesus served the Disciples.

> *"But from everlasting to everlasting, the Lord's love is with those who fear him, and his righteousness with their children's children."* (Psalms 103:17 NIV)

Business Associates

Let our business dealings be dictated by scriptural truths that function by faith in God and His Word. This will allow God's blessings to flow into our life and business and will be an opportunity to give glory to God. Lost business men and women will take notice and will want to know our secret for success.

> *"Trust in the Lord with all thine heart; and lean not unto thine own understanding. In all thy ways acknowledge him, and he shall direct thy paths."* (Proverbs 3:5–6 KJV)

Church Family

The church is God's plan for the gospel to be preached, for His love to be displayed, and for people to be sent into the lost world with the good news of Jesus. It is not an option for the Christ follower to be separated from other believers. It is in this loving, spiritual family relationship that our lives are enriched and we are sent on our God-given mission.

> *"So then you are no longer strangers and aliens, but you are fellow citizens with the saints and members of the household of God, built on the foundation of the apostles and prophets, Christ Jesus himself being the cornerstone, in whom the whole structure, being joined together, grows into a holy temple in the Lord. In Him you also are being built together into a dwelling place for God by the Spirit."* (Ephesians 2:19–22 ESV)

Friends and Neighbors

Be Jesus to those you live around. Live with integrity in the small things and big things. Be a friend even to those who are difficult and pray for the influence of Christ to flow through you to reach them for His Kingdom. Jesus gave all His followers the same instruction:

> *"You are like salt for everyone on earth. But if salt no longer tastes like salt, how can it make food salty? All it is good for is to be thrown out and walked on.*
>
> *You are like light for the whole world. A city built on top of a hill cannot be hidden, and no one would light a lamp and put it under a clay pot. A lamp is placed on a lampstand, where it can give light to everyone in the house. Make your*

light shine, so that others will see the good that you do and will praise your Father in heaven." (Matthew 5:13–16 CEV)

People Around the World

One of the challenges Jesus gave His followers was to take the good news of salvation through Jesus Christ to all people around the world.

> *"Go therefore and make disciples of all nations, baptizing them in the name of the Father and of the Son and of the Holy Spirit, teaching them to observe all that I have commanded you. And behold, I am with you always, to the end of the age."* (Matthew 28:19–20 ESV)

Go on mission opportunities when you can and as the Lord leads, and support mission efforts in sacrificial financial offerings so that others can go.

6. Miraculous Finances

There are really only two ways to deal with finances in life. One way is under the control of ourselves (self-god). The other is to handle them as the God of the universe directs. If we do it His way, there are immeasurable benefits.

7. Joy In Trials

> *"Count it all joy, my brothers, when you meet trials of various kinds, for you know that the testing of your faith produces steadfastness. And let steadfastness have its full effect, that you may be perfect and complete, lacking in nothing."* (James 1:2–4 ESV)

The trials that we face in this life are tools in the hands of our mighty God. Notice it says, "The testing of your faith" is what develops perseverance. The Word says it is that very discomfort that would have brought a great and Godly work in our lives if we had simply remained. Instead, we often run off to another fellowship of believers before God can do His work. Because of this, we are prone to the same process in our new church. Notice what will happen if we don't persevere in a trial:

- Perseverance will not finish its work because we ran.
- We would not become mature, we would remain incomplete, and we would lack many important things.

My challenge to you is the same as James'. Look at the next trial in your life as an opportunity to rejoice in the Lord and know that He is doing something in you. Look at it as a place where the Lord is growing you into something greater. Don't run from the trial; plant your feet and remain. Let God finish His work in you with the tool of discomfort. As you persevere, God will develop maturity in you, and you will become more complete in Him. Let's remain where God planted us. Let's stay long enough in one place for our roots to grow deep and our life to bear much fruit.

Let's Talk or Think About It

- Do you think that living the abundant life that God talks about happens only when we go to heaven, or do you thing that we can also live in the Lord's abundance here and now?

- In this book I have listed seven areas that I believe make up the core issues of life. If we live these core issues under the Lordship of Christ, the blessings that occur let us live the abundant life while here on this earth. Can you think of other important areas that also could or should be added to this list?

- Of the seven issues listed, in which ones do you feel that you are living in God's promised abundance?

- In which ones do you feel you are still wandering in a desert place? Why?

- What has God spoken to you about while you read through this book? What are you planning on doing about what He has shown you?

CHAPTER 15

"Final Thoughts"

─────────────────────────────────────

I want to thank you for taking your valuable time to walk through this study from a place of bondage to a life of abundance with me. It is an honor to know that you have dedicated this much effort to finding your freedom in Jesus.

The process of this book starts with the premise of John 8:36, *"So if the Son sets you free, you will be free indeed."*

It starts with this truth of freedom because it is important for us to know that the Lord Jesus wants people to live in His freedom. To live in a place where we are no longer bound by curses, lies and deceptions that have been imprinted on our life ultimately by Satan himself. In this book we have walked through the steps to freedom. To help us remember the steps let me restate them here.

Step #1 Understand that bondage is the desire of the enemy (Satan) to steal, kill and destroy our life.

Step #2 Identify the bondages that have attached to our life. We do this by focusing on those concepts in our mind that were planted to distort our thinking and cause us to live under the negative influences of fear, doubt, shame, and guilt.

Step #3 Realize that the person or situation which planted the bondage in our life is not the problem. Satan uses people and even our own sinful choices to bring in his condemnation. This is the area that Jesus emphasizes the importance of learning to forgive those who have brought damage into our life. Forgiving others allows us to be forgiven as well.

Step #4 Once the bondages are identified we are able to go to Jesus, the one who paid for all of our sin and condemnation by His death on the cross. By faith we ask the Lord to remove from our life all of the demonic attachments. He is all-powerful and will use His Kingly position to order all of Satan's tactics to be removed. He will set you free!

Step #5 We now begin the process of transforming our minds. Once the fear, doubt, shame, guilt and curses are removed we must now fill our minds with truth. The Apostle Paul described the process like this, *"Do not be conformed any longer to the pattern of this world, but be transformed by the renewing of your mind. Then you will be able to test and approve what God's will is - His good, pleasing and perfect will."* (Romans 12:2 NIV)

Step #6 Start learning to live by the truths and promises of God as revealed in scripture. As we begin to obey the Lord as instructed in His Word, the blessings of the Lord begin to flow into our life. This by definition is "the blessed life."

Step #7 Walk in the Lord Jesus' freedom and truth. Begin to represent HIS Kingdom. Scripture says, *"We are therefore Christ's ambassadors, as though God were making His appeal through us. We implore you on Christ's behalf: Be reconciled to God."* (II Corinthians 5:20 NIV)

It is my prayer that this process will help you and your loved ones through some difficult days and out from under the bondages that this world attaches to our lives.

This process is still hard for me, and I often feel like a beginner. I want you to know that it is ok if you are not in the place you feel like you should be spiritually. God always meets us where we are and lovingly leads us through this spiritual journey all the way to His promised freedom. In the words of Central Christian Church in Las Vegas,

"It's OK to not be OK."

The Apostle Paul said it like this when he was nearing the end of his spiritual journey:

> *"Brothers, I do not consider that I have made it my own. But one thing I do: forgetting what lies behind and straining forward to what lies ahead, I press on toward the goal for the prize of the upward call of God in Christ Jesus."* (Philippians 3:13–14 ESV)

What does Paul say is the first step toward the prize of the Lord?

Paul lays out the steps for how we are to move into God's Promised Land.

1. We must forget what is behind.

Everyone can live under massive condemnation and guilt for the dumb, hurtful, and sinful things we have done in our lives. Perhaps we may be bitter about what someone else did to us. The Lord knows that if we continue in self-doubt or unforgiveness, we could live our entire lives trapped as slaves to these bondages and thoughts. Forgetting what is behind is an easy thing to say, but please understand that it is not really possible to forget our failures, bondages, and the lies of the enemy. Paul was simply saying that we are to make a decision to not look back in grief and remorse. Once the Lord has covered our sins and we exercise forgiveness for others, and ourselves we can be set free from the past.

Why do you think that forgetting what is behind is important?

Do you think it is really possible to "forget" the awful and traumatic events of our past?

What do you think Paul meant when he said to forget what is behind?

2. We must press on toward the prize.

What is the prize? For me, it is living in the freedom and abundance the Lord has provided for us. But the key is pressing on. Don't give up when you find that you are disappointed in your behavior or if someone else does not live up to your expectations. Get up and press on toward the goal: the high calling of Jesus Christ. He would not have made a promise if He was unable to fulfill it.

What is the second step Paul says is necessary to move us forward toward the prize of the Lord?

What is the Prize for which the Lord has called us heavenward?

It would be my delight to hear from you if the Lord used this information to help you along your spiritual journey. You can email me at mark@ stonebridgenixa.com to share your testimony.

My prayer is that we find His full freedom so that we will be a light in the midst of a darkening world and salt that will bring the flavoring and preservation of Christ into our decaying environment. Enjoy the freedoms and full benefits that come from living in God's Promised Land.

Mark Killingsworth
Senior Pastor
Stonebridge Church, Nixa, MO

SECTION #5

Small Group Leader's Guide

A Captive No More

Small Group Leader's Guide

SESSION 1:
"Understanding Bondage"

Open with Prayer

Introduction
Do an icebreaker game for group members to become familiar with one another and remember names. An example would be to have each group member pair up with a person they know the least and do the following:

- Introduce yourself.
- Learn your new friend's name.
- Find out something about this person that makes them memorable.

Then, come back together and have each pair introduce one other to the group, including the person's name and something memorable they have learned.

How would you summarize what you learned in Chapter 1 of our book study?

Give a few minutes for people to get their memories working. But this will bring everyone's attention to the point of the first chapter.

What is bondage?

The book defines it as, "…a condition of servitude to someone or something from which the person in bondage has no personal power to find freedom." It is the result of sin. It may be sin I have committed or a sin committed against me by someone else.

What were some of the bondages discussed in the chapter?

Jaycee Lee Dugard's bondage to Phillip Garrido, drinking, gambling, pornography, overeating, fear, finances

Do you think that bondage can develop in our lives through the following activities?

- A word curse spoken into our life by someone important to us
- A rejection by a father or a mother
- Early exposure to alcohol or drugs

SESSION 2:
"A False Belief Is Planted"

Open with Prayer

Introduction
Tonight as you gather, greet everyone and let them know that you are honored that they chose to invest this time. Share with them your expectation that God is going to move in some exciting ways that will help us be captives no more.

Review Chapter 1 Main Points

Losing Vision
A danger grows as we move further from the original vision of faith that our forefathers developed from the truths of Scripture.

Does anyone see the danger for America as we get further and further from the original intent of our founding fathers? Give time for discussion.

Complacency in Prosperity
When a Godly vision is established and fought for, the blessings of God always follow. But what happens to the generations that get to enjoy the prosperity without the sacrifices necessary to win and keep the freedoms? For example, what has happened to the American culture now, 200 years away from the original vision? Give time for discussion.

Selfishness Creates Room for the Enemy
Many times, out of prosperity develops a sense of entitlement—the feeling that we deserve this prosperity. We demand our freedoms. As entitlement grows, a sense of dependency also develops. In our dependent state, we start giving in to a master.

Does anyone see how this is illustrated in the current condition of America?

Freedom Dies, Slavery Ensues

What happens to a person or even a nation when there is the loss of freedom? It is always followed by bondage. If the American Constitutional Republic fails, what do you believe will come in behind that failure? Give time for discussion.

Overview Chapter 2
Discuss how a false belief can be planted into a mind that can cause us to become captives.

Talk about the power of the word to bless or to curse, to bring life or death.

Bible Study

To strengthen this concept, let's do a study together out of Judges 6. We are going to look at a man who had a poor view of himself and attempt to see how he developed this demonic deception of weakness.

Read Judges 6:1–16. (Walk through the verses)

Verse 1: What does sin (rebellion against God) do on a spiritual level?

God gave them into the hands of their enemy.

Verse 2: Midianites represent the "Slave Master." They have an oppressive power.

Verses 3–4: What does a Satanic force do to our livelihood?

It steals our provision.

Verse 5: Sin unleashes a swarm of locusts that come in to destroy everything.

Verses 6–10: God's plan for helping people out of a demonic attack and bondage.

It starts when we cry out to the Lord. God sent His Word. He reveals "I Am the one who sets you free." I Am the one who snatches you from the oppressor. I Am the one who prepares the way for you. I Am your God, and you are to worship me alone.

Verse 11: What was Gideon's condition?

Hiding in a wine press. Living in great fear of the enemy.

Verse 12: How did God see Gideon?

A Mighty Warrior

Verse 13: A question many Christ followers ask is, "If God is with us then why do bad things happen? Where is the God of deliverance when I need Him? I really feel that God has abandoned me!"

Verse 14: What was the Lord's response to these questions?

Go in the strength you have and save Israel.

Verse 15: What was Gideon's self-concept?

Weakest and least

Verse 16: Does God accept His self-concept?

No. He says, "I will be with you. You will strike down all the Midianites."

What did you learn about the power of words? Someone read John 10:10-15. Ask these questions.

- Who is the thief?
- What is his purpose?
- What is the purpose of the Good Shepherd for your life?
- As the Good Shepherd, what does He do for us, His sheep?
- What feelings and thoughts do you have about this reality?

SESSION 3:
"A Controlling Power Is Allowed"

Open with Prayer

Review

During **week 1,** we looked at a picture of bondage. We found a good definition, "A condition of servitude to someone or something from which the person in bondage has no personal power to find freedom." We also started to identify some possible areas of bondage that may be hindering us personally.

During **week 2**, we saw how words can be spoken into a life that can cause a curse. Sometimes a curse can hinder and define our lives in very powerful ways. During this week, we risked looking inward to see if we can identify any curses that have harmed us.

What is the formula that this chapter revealed as to how a spoken word becomes an action?

Words become ideas Ideas become belief Belief becomes action

As you read Dylan Klebold's journal, what did you see that would cause you to think that he had allowed a controlling power into his life?

What do you think happens to people who begin to identify with and define themselves by an area of bondage?

They are being controlled by a deception of the enemy to steal, kill, and destroy their lives.

Can anyone in the group identify a word curse that has been spoken into their life? Would anyone feel safe enough to share with us the curse that has been like a slave master to you? (Let several share as time allows. As each person shares, ask the following questions.)

- How was that curse planted in your life?
- What thoughts accompanied the original curse?
- How did those thoughts grow into an idea in your mind?
- Did that curse grow into a belief within you that may have been a hindrance in your life?
- What reinforced the curse that caused you to accept the deception as truth?
- How has this idea affected your behavior and choices?

Read Exodus 5:6–9 with the group and see if you can discover all of the things that happen when we are fully under the deception that has us in bondage.

> They had lost their God-given vision of being a privileged people designed by Him to be a blessing to the entire human race. As bondage gains control of a people or a life the labor associated with that bondage gets harder. Slave drivers demand more and more without mercy. After a while, the slave cannot see himself as anything but a slave.

Bible Study
Read Matthew 17:14–21 and consider the following questions:

What were the symptoms of the son?
Suffering and seizures

Why do you think the Disciples could not heal him?
Verse 20 says "little faith."

How did Jesus deal with the sickness of the son?
He identified it as the work of a demon and rebuked the demon?

If we take Jesus' answer about having mountain-moving faith, what are we to be able to do as Ambassadors of God's Kingdom?
Read Matthew 8:10 and compare what 'great faith' can do in comparison to what 'little faith' could not do.

What did Jesus say was the limitation for His followers?

Nothing will be impossible.

If we truly believe Matthew 17:21, how will this change the way we deal with demonic lies, ideas, beliefs, and actions?

SESSION 4:
"When Bondage is Complete"

Open with Prayer

Review
During **week 1**, we looked at a picture of bondage. We found a good definition, "A condition of servitude to someone or something from which the person in bondage has no personal power to find freedom." We also started to identify some possible areas of bondage that may be hindering us personally.

During **week 2**, we saw how words can be spoken into a life that can cause a curse. Sometimes a curse can hinder and define our lives in very powerful ways. During this week, we risked looking inward to see if we could identify any curses that have harmed us.

During **week 3**, we considered the bondage formula: a word curse is spoken that turns into an idea; that idea then develops into a belief; then the belief turns into action. A few of our group members shared how they had personally experienced some form of this formula working to harm them. We considered some of the negative things that happen when a person becomes self-identified by a curse.

Discussion Questions
Let's look at the first time a demonic deception is revealed in Scripture. Turn to Genesis 2:15–17 and read together.

What were God's instructions and intentions for mankind?
Now look at Genesis 3:1-5 and make note of how Satan introduced deception.

What tools did Satan use to tempt Eve and Adam to sin?
He used doubt, lies, and a temptation to become god of their own life. The bottom line of all sin is self-rule.

160

What are the biggest areas in your life where demonic deception causes you to doubt God?

If Satan is successful in getting a person to doubt God, self-rule takes over. What are some areas of your life where you find yourself attempting to control and in essence push God out?

In Romans 1, the Apostle Paul paints a clear picture of what happens when a person chooses self-rule and rejects God. In the book, read chapter 1 of Romans and walk through the seven steps to a reprobate mind.

Based on the levels of bondage discussed, what level do you find yourself in? (use Romans chapter 1 as your guide)

SESSION 5:
"When the Worst Becomes the Best"

Open with Prayer

It would be helpful for you as the leader of your small group to share a time in your life where you came to a very difficult place and there the Lord had a life changing impact on your life. If you don't feel comfortable in doing this personally then see if you can find a story or testimony of someone who has experienced God's best in the place where they were experiencing the worst.

Have you experienced a turning point in your life?" (Allow a couple to share their experience.)

In this chapter, the pastor who wrote this book shared with you a personal testimony of a turning point that happened in his life just a few years ago at the church he pastored. He attempted to capture the level of pain that he experienced during that time but had trouble finding words that could describe it.

At his lowest point, he even asked God to take him home. He said, "I could not take the hurt anymore." It was in that pain that God started to speak clearly.

Why do you think God spoke those four statements to this pastor at this desperate point in his life?

"Take your hands off My church, and I will build My Church so that even the gates of hell will not be able to prevail against it."

"Seek first the Kingdom of God and His righteousness and all these things will be given you."

"I am sovereign God and I Am in charge of all things."

"I am going to fulfill Psalm 23 in your life."

Why do you think the story of Amari was a turning point in the church? Do you think God provides a turning point for everyone?

What life-changing message did you receive from God when you were lying flat on your back at the bottom of your pit?

Read Exodus 5:22-6:8 and list or share with your small group what God shows you when you get to a TURNING POINT.

Why do you think God allows us to get to this "end of the rope" experience in our life?

What is it about humanity that requires this awful TURNING POINT experience before we get our life right with our Creator? (Use Ephesians 2 for a guideline)

SESSION 6:
"Where a Redeemer Is Found"

Open with prayer

Introduction
Start out your group with some food and fellowship time. Remember, real and deepening relationships are the environment where true-life change happens.

Bible Study
Read Exodus 3:1–10. Then ask the following questions for discussion:

Who was Moses before God spoke to him?
Shepherd of sheep

What do we learn about God in this scripture?
Here are some possible answers:

> *He knows the oppression and bondage each person is in.*
> *He hears the cries that come from people's distress.*
> *He is aware of our suffering.*
> *He desires for enslaved people to be set free and provides a way out of bondage.*
> *He has a plan for each person to find full life in Jesus.*
> *He has a plan to use redeemed people to help others out of their bondage.*

What stories come to mind of times that God called people out of their normal life to function as a redeemer or leader?

Let's Start with the Old Testament:

Some possible answers:

- *Gideon (Jud. 6–8)*
- *Joseph (Gen. 30–49)*
- *David (II Sam)*
- *Moses (Exodus)*
- *Hezekiah (II Chron. 29)*
- *Daniel (Daniel)*
- *All the Prophets*

Now let's move to the New Testament:

Some possible answers:

- *The Disciples*
- *Saul to Paul (Conversion in Acts)*
- *Peter (Vision that sent him to the Gentiles)*
- *The Church (Acts 2)*
- *The gifts of the Holy Spirit (I Cor. 12, Rom. 12)*

Any current-day people you have known?

Some possible answers:

- *Billy Graham*
- *Chuck Swindoll*
- *Chuck Smith*

Is there a time you have had a burning bush type of experience?

Who were most of these people before God/Jesus called them to follow Him?

Some possible answers:

1. *Moses, a shepherd*
2. *Gideon, a scared and weak person*
3. *Joseph, an irritating younger brother*
4. *David, a young shepherd*
5. *The disciples were a mixture of backgrounds*
6. *Fishermen*
7. *Tax collector*
8. *Physician*
9. *Common men*
10. *Normal, common, everyday people just like you and me*

Does God still call normal, everyday people to the role leading others out of bondage? How does He do that?

Why did Jesus have such harsh words for the Pharisees of His day?
Possibly because they were religious rule keepers and felt they were superior to others.

Why did sinners feel comfortable with Jesus?
Possible answer: He didn't judge or condemn them. He loved them. He forgave them. He showed them a better way for their life.

Why do many people outside of Christianity look at following Christ as a way to make their life less fun?

Some possible answers:

1. *Because they feel the Bible is full of do's and a lot of don'ts.*
2. *Because some Christ followers have become more like Pharisees than like Jesus. Why?*

What reaches people better? A strong, nearly perfect person or a transparent person who reveals their own brokenness?

What does it take to be a "Moses": a leader that helps people find true freedom in Jesus?

> *Possible answer: Most people feel that they could never really be someone like Moses because they feel that it is their job to lead everyone to the Lord, show them how to be saved, get them baptized, get them to church, and get them to be a good Christ follower. They are overwhelmed to the point that paralysis sets in.*

What if we made it much simpler? What if being a Moses was simply seeing each relationship that the Lord brings across your path today as an opportunity to love them like Jesus did?

Examples:
- *A word of encouragement*
- *A time to listen*
- *A prayer lifting their need to the Lord*
- *A helping hand*
- *A financial gift to help in time of need*
- *A Godly counsel to help them move in the right direction*
- *An invitation to join us in worship*
- *Kindness in an unkind world*

What are some current "higher powers" offered by this world?

What happens when we put our faith and trust in false promises, false gods, or idols?

Moses was an Old Testament redeemer. How was he like the redeemer of the New Testament, which is Jesus Christ?

What are you trusting in as the redeemer for your life and why?

SESSION 7:
"Where a Leap of Faith Is Required"

Open with Prayer

Introduction and Review
Tonight marks the halfway point in our journey through the book.

In the first 4 chapters, we looked closely at what bondage really is, how it starts, and how it develops. In chapters 5 and 6, we saw that usually there must be a "turning point" in life before we really see our need for a redeemer.

This evening, we begin to search for a redeemer. First, review the eleven false redeemers discussed in the book.

Bible Study
Using the Old Testament temple as a picture, show the reality of a person who is "dead in trespass and sin."

Outer Court: Represents our bodies. Scripture says the average life span for a man is three score and 10, or seventy years.

Holy Place: Represents our souls. Paul describes the soul in three parts:

1. Mind (Thinker)
2. Will (Chooser)
3. Emotion (Feeler)

This part of man is eternal, with two possible destinations after the body dies. Hell is for Satan, the demons, and all who reject Jesus as Savior and Master. Heaven is for those who have accepted Jesus' payment for our sin and Lordship of their lives.

Holy of Holies: Represents our spirits. See Rom. 3:23, Rom. 6:23, and John 3. Rulership of your life is determined here.

- Self-rulership: Process and destination are revealed in Romans 1.
- Some other god/idol: A false belief does not bring release from sin's bondage.
- Holy Spirit: The spirit was designed to be ruled by the Holy Spirit.

Those who acknowledge their sinfulness and hopelessness and believe in Jesus the Messiah shall be born again. These people will go to heaven when their physical bodies die.

What are some of the ways you have tried to find answers and meaning that left you empty?

What were the results of your search in pursuing a false redeemer?

How did God get His message of salvation to you?

What were the fears you had to move past?

What could we do practically that would help people who have entered the Wide Gate and the Broad Road that is leading them toward destruction?

How did you discover that Jesus is the Messiah (redeemer)? Tell us what God used to get His message of salvation to you?

What was your leap of faith like for you? What were the fears you had to move past?

Break into Small Groups: (15 min.)

Take Matthew 7:13-14 and see if you can discover what Jesus was revealing about salvation and redemption in these verses.

Large Group Share Time

What did your group discover about...

- The narrow gate
- The wide gate
- The broad road
- The narrow road

Why do you think only a few find the narrow gate and road?

What practical ways could we help those who have entered the wide gate and the broad road?

SESSION 8:
"Where All Things Become New"

Open with Prayer

Read the opening paragraph of the book in chapter 8.

Based on Scripture, what is God's intention for His people? What does the Promised Land concept look like for modern Christ followers?

Some possible answers:

- *A powerful picture of living in God's blessing (Deut. 28:1-14)*
- *Filled with the Spirit and experiencing the fruit of the Spirit (Gal. 5:22–23)*
- *Experiencing life to the fullest (John 10:10b)*
- *Freedom (II Cor. 3:17 and Rom. 8:21)*
- *A transformed mind (Rom. 12:2)*
- *Living under God's blessing (Pr. 28:25)*
- *Prospering in what we do (Ps. 1:3)*

Based on Genesis 1:26–30, what was God's full intention for man's life?

Some possible answers:

- *To rule over creation*
- *To rule from a perspective that God is the Creator*
- *For the man and woman to produce children that grow up under the knowledge that God is the Creator*
- *Man's diet originally was more vegetarian.*

What do you think it means that we were created in the image of God?

Some possible answers:

- *Three-part nature of God*
- *Ambassadors of Jesus*
- *A part of the body of Christ*

What caused God's plan for mankind to get off track?

SESSION 9:
"The Transformed Mind"

Open with Prayer

This is the ninth week of our journey to being "A Captive No More." We are now at the *post-salvation* stage. We have chosen Jesus as our Redeemer, we have been forgiven, we have been in-dwelt with the Holy Spirit, and now we start on the journey to God's Abundance.

Group Activity

Choose three people to stand and read three different verses of scripture all at the same time. Then ask the group the following questions:

- What did you hear? *words, noise, no real clear message*
- What did you feel? *frustrated and confused*
- What was wrong? *conflicting messages*

One of the most important skills we must develop on this spiritual journey is to learn to identify the voices that attempt to gain our attention and get us to take action on their wishes for our lives.

Bible Study
Scripture reveals that there are three major competing voices:

- The voice of our flesh
- The voice of the demonic
- The voice of God

Read the second paragraph of page 51 in the book: "In their mind they still see themselves as slaves..."

Read Exodus 14:8–12. Look for the thought process of the Israelites when they encountered difficulty on their road to freedom.

- They were terrified.
- They cried out to the Lord.
- They complained to Moses (their leader).
- They said that the journey was going to kill them and that they should have stayed in bondage.

What do we do when we face a difficult place in our journey to the Lord's Abundance?

A Challenge: "Do not conform any longer to the pattern of this world, but be transformed by the renewing of your mind. Then you will be able to test and approve what God's will is—His good, pleasing and perfect will." (Rom. 12:2)

A Warning: "He was a murderer from the beginning, not holding to the truth, for there is not truth in him. When he lies, he speaks his native language, for he is a liar and the father of lies." (John 8:44)

How Do We Identify the Demonic Voice?

- When the message steals, kills, or destroys (John 10:10)
- When God's truth is hard to understand (Matt. 13:19)
- When the message condemns (John 3:17)
- When the message is a curse (Prov. 18:21)
- When the message leads us from the Lord and brings fear (John 8:44)
- When there is demonic oppression (Matt. 17:18)
- When confusion comes that removes peace (I Cor. 14:33)

How Do We Identify the Fleshly Voice?

- When our pride makes us feel better than someone else (Matt. 16:6)

- When we are tempted to make sin decisions based upon lust, greed, or pride (I John 2:15–17

  Lust: Desires of the flesh, sexual sin
  Greed: Desires of the eyes
  Pride: Confidence in possessions

How Do We Identify the Voice of God?

- Find clarity and direction in God's Word. (Ps. 119:105)
- Be clear and committed to truth. (John 14:6)
- Dwell in God's Word. (Col. 3:16)
- Be committed in a healthy church. (Acts. 2:42)
- Grow in faith by hearing God's Word. (Rom. 10:17)

Once you get God's Word on a subject, these are the actions to take:

- Prepare your mind for action. (I Pet. 11:12)
- Begin living as a new creation. (II Cor. 5:17)
- Start believing in your God-given purpose. (I Cor. 12:4–7)
- Advance toward your life of abundance. (John 10:10)

Small Group Questions

What satanic deceptions have been the hardest for you to overcome?

How have those deceptions hurt and hindered your life?

Were you able to find scriptures that counteract the deceptions? How do these help you become transformed?

If you find yourself in bondage to a deception or a curse, we would be willing to gather around you this evening and pray a prayer of faith asking the Lord to come and set you free and to give you Kingdom energy to move toward freedom.

SESSION 10:
"Overcoming Fear With Faith"

Open with Prayer

Introduction
As we have learned so far in this study, what are the primary tools Satan uses to drive and manipulate people toward bondage?

Possible answers: Lies, deception, fear

Bible Study
The stories of Israel's journey out of bondage and the subsequent experiences as they moved toward the land of promise reveal several areas of life where fear will attempt to overtake us.

Have group members look up and read the following scriptures. As they read, ask the group to listen for the lie, the deception, or the fear that Satan was using to attempt their defeat. After each scripture is read, give the group a chance to explain the challenge that Israel faced in that circumstance.

Exodus 14:9–12   *Fear of falling back under old bondages*
Exodus 15:22–24   *Fear of facing life difficulties*
Exodus 16:1–3   *Fear of not having enough*
Exodus 17:8–9   *Fear of being overtaken by an old slave master*

Possibly one of the greatest fears Israel faced—and that we continue to face today—occurs when God asks us to become conquering Christ followers instead of simple followers who are constantly on the defensive.

Using the story of the 12 spies sent into the Promised Land, compare the two different responses to the challenge of moving into a land of abundance.

The Fear Response: (Numbers 13:26-29) Have someone read the passage and then spend some time talking about how they responded in fear and the result of that decision.

The Faith Response: (Numbers 14:6-9) Have someone read the passage and then spend some time talking about how these two responded in faith and how they came to that position.

The Big Questions
This is a turning point for this study; so give time for discussion, insight, and the revelation of the Holy Spirit as you ask these questions.

What is the difference in the way the two groups responded when challenged by God to go in and take possession of the land?
The group of ten focused on the bigness of the challenges before them while Joshua and Caleb focused on the character and promise of God.

What did Joshua and Caleb know or do differently than the ten spies who said they could not go into the land promised by God?

What is the difference between wandering in the desert for 40 years because of a fear choice and crossing into the Promised Land by faith?

This is the KEY REVELATION of moving into the land of abundance Jesus promises to His people. Living in the desert of disobedience and fear keeps us living in a position of DEFENSE. God brought Israel through the desert and several very challenging events in order to build their faith. Each event was something that came against them so that they had to learn to depend upon God. He never failed them. But at the crossing into the land of promise, God was asking His people to stop living in DEFENSE and start living in OFFENSE—To stop being followers and wanderers and to become conquerors.

How do we overcome the controlling power of fear in our lives?

Read Eph. 6:16—*"Above all else, take up the shield of faith."*

Now read the story of the Spartans and their commitment to raising warriors. Begin reading on page 61 at the second paragraph. It begins, "I read a story in college..."

If we were carving our "Shield of Faith" today, what would be the biblical verses you would want to stake your very life upon?

Here are some great scriptural promises to suggest if your group has trouble identifying what they should write on their shield—

II Timothy 1:7, Galatians 2:20, Jeremiah 29:11, Exodus 15:2, Colossians 2:9, James 4:7, Galatians 5:1, Proverbs 4:23, Philippians 4:19, I John 4:4, Romans 8:28, Psalm 27, Psalm 91, Ephesians 3:20, Psalm 40, Isaiah 41:13-16, Exodus 14:14, Psalm 3, James 1:22, Psalm 84:11

SESSION 11:
"The Road Less Traveled"

Open with Prayer

Introduction
We have discovered many things during this book study. One of the most important truths that we have uncovered is this:

It matters what you believe.

Why does it matter so much what you believe?

> *Because the decisions we make in our lives are based upon what we believe. If what we believe is wrong, our decisions will be wrong. But if our decisions are based upon truth, this will help us live the life of freedom that Jesus promised.*

Bible Study
Lead a discussion based on the information that is found in Chapter 11.

In Matthew 7:13–14, Jesus shows the reality of decisions we make. Let's read those verses and see if we can answer the following questions:

What if the wide gate and the broad road are chosen by fear?

What are the results of this choice?

> *It ends in destruction.*

Let's go back and read Numbers 13:27–33, where 10 of the 12 Jewish spies made their decision based upon fear. From what you learned in chapter 11, what are the consequences of decisions based upon fear?

- *Fear hides the presence, power, and promise of God. (Exodus 6:6–8)*
- *Fearfully made decisions have painful consequences. (Numbers 14:27–34)*

- *Fear has a god, and its name is Mammon (Money). (Matthew 6:24)*

What if the small gate is Jesus and the narrow road is the road of faith? What happens on this narrow road?

Only a few find it, but it leads to life.

Now let's remind ourselves how faith worked for Joshua and Caleb when they decided to trust God and go in to take the land. Read Exodus 6:6–8.

What can we learn by looking at the faith of Joshua and Caleb?

Some possible answers:

- *Faith sees God as greater than the current challenge.*
- *Faith brings deliverance.*
- *A formula for faith that works: Stand firm and do not run, Do not be impressed with the challenge, Focus on the superiority of God, Listen and obey the Word of God, Experience the victory.*
- *Faith brings peace. (Mark 4:39)*
- *Faith brings God into the crisis.*

SESSION 12:
"The Crossing"

Open with Prayer

A Powerful Word from the Lord

The thing that changes when Christ followers choose to walk in the land of promise, of which Jesus described as "life that is more abundant," is that He wants us to move from a position of spiritual defense to a position of spiritual offense.

After coming out of slavery in Egypt, the entire journey from bondage to God's promise was filled with events that caused Israel to live on the defense. In these events, challenges came to them that were too big for them to handle. These challenges included being chased by their old slave life, being trapped by a sea that hindered their escape, and experiencing food and water shortages in the desert. But time after time, God showed His guidance, His provision, and His faithfulness. The journey was designed to build up their faith that their God would never fail them. An established faith was necessary for the biggest step that still lied in front of them.

That final and biggest faith step was to stop acting in a defensive manner and to move to a position of offense based upon knowing God and trusting His Word.

- To move from being a follower To being a conqueror.
- To move from being a complainer To being a proclaimer.
- To move from speaking fear To speaking faith.
- To move from reacting to challenges To walking in confidence.
- To move from fear motivations To faith positions.
- To move from manna survival To abundant living.
- To move from being a slave To being a giant slayer.
- To move from trusting only self To trusting fully in the Lord.
- To move from being terrified To living in peace.

- To move from being a person who says "No way" To being a person who says "Yes Sir."
- To move from being people who give up To being people who persevere.
- To move from wandering as nomads To carrying shields as warriors.

Bible Study

Three big challenges stand in our way as we enter God's Abundance:

The Challenge of Crossing the Jordan
(Joshua 3:11–13, 3:17)

What are the lessons we need to learn from Israel when it comes to entering in?

The Covenant or Word of the Lord must lead.
The Leader of the family must lead the way.
Your step of faith into the water stops its power.

What could be the Jordan (thing that hinders you) that keeps you from entering into God's abundant life? (This might be a controlling deception or a remaining bondage. Let the group share their hindrances.)

The Presence of Giants
(Genesis 6:1–4)

What are some of the giants we may face in our day that threaten us from living in God's abundance? Allow the group to share what they see as "giants in the land."

A secularized government moving toward socialism
The Americanized church that turns Christianity into a "me-focused" experience

The Hindrance of Walled Cities
(Numbers 13:26–28)

What are some of the possible strong hindrances that would keep us from possessing the abundance of the Lord? Allow the group to share ideas.

Demonic strongholds that remain hooked into our lives
Disapproval or rejection by religious people
Increasing social pressure to reject Jesus

Remember what Caleb said when he faced these things: "Then Caleb silenced the people before Moses and said, "We should go up and take possession of the land, for we can certainly do it" (Numbers 13:30 NIV).

SESSION 13:
"Hearing, Knowing, and Following God's Voice"

Open with Prayer

Introduction

Why do you think the following statement this book made a few chapters ago is correct?

It matters what you believe.

If we add the following scriptural revelations to this statement, how does its meaning change?

"He (Satan) was a murderer from the beginning, not holding to the truth, for there is not truth in him. When he lies, he speaks his native language, for he is a liar and the father of lies." (John 8:44)

Jesus said, "Watch out that no one deceives you. For many will come in My name, claiming, 'I am the Christ,' and will deceive many." (Matthew 24:4–5)

"For false prophets will appear and perform great signs and miracles to deceive even the elect—if that were possible." (Matthew 24:24)

Bible Study
Matthew 13:3–23

What is the "hard soil" type of person like?

What is the "rocky soil" type of person like?

What is the "thorny soil" type of person like?

What is the "good soil" type of person like?

The author used two different illustrations of common life issues to attempt to clarify how these soils respond to the seed of God's Word.

What were your thoughts about the tithe and the different responses?

What were your thoughts about the issue of husband and wife responsibilities?

The author made some suggestions about how God may speak to those who want to hear His communications. Which method or methods does God most often use to speak to you?

God Speaks through the following:

- Reading Scripture
- Prayer
- People
- Creation
- Holy Spirit
- Visions and dreams

SESSION 14:
"Living In God's Promise"

Open with Prayer

Introduction

Proverbs 29:18 is a power-packed verse. This is what it says in a variety of translations:

> *Where there is no revelation, the people cast off restraint, but blessed is he who keeps the law.* (NIV)

> *Where there is no vision, the people perish. But he that keepeth the law, happy is he.* (KJV)

> *Where there is no prophetic vision, the people cast off restraint, but blessed is he who keeps the law.* (ESV)

The primary meaning of this verse is that unless humans hear the Divine message from God's Word, they have no understanding of truth. This results in social chaos.

To apply this verse to this study of "A Captive No More," it is important that we have a scriptural revelation about what it means to live the "abundant life" that Jesus promised in John 10:10b—"I have come that they may have life, and have it to the full."

What do you think is the vision of the life that Jesus wants for His people? What does "abundant life" mean?

Bible Study

In Chapter 14, the author has suggested seven major areas of life that, when lived according to a scriptural vision, allow for living in the Promised Land.

Walk through each of the seven areas as a group.

1. A Born-Again Spirit
2. A Transformed Soul
3. A Spirit-Empowered Life
4. Clear Life Mission
5. God-Based Relationships
6. Miraculous Finances
7. Joy in Trials

Small Group Discussion
Allow everyone to share their personal victory areas and challenge areas.

Pray specifically for challenging areas in people's lives. Ask the Lord to send His strength in these areas and to help us move into His abundance.

SESSION 15:
"Final Thoughts"

Open with Prayer

Introduction
Tonight marks the end of our small group journey through the book, "A Captive No More."

Discuss how the Lord has worked in each person's life as your group has journeyed closely together through this study over the last 14 weeks.

Bible Study

> *"Brothers, I do not consider myself yet to have taken hold of it. But one thing I do: forgetting what is behind and straining toward what is ahead, I press on toward the goal to win the prize for which God has called me heavenward in Christ Jesus."* (Philippians 3:13–14)

What does Paul say is the first step toward the prize of the Lord?
Forgetting what is behind

Why do you think that forgetting what is behind is important?
Things like the following cause us to live in bondage: sin, failure, shame, guilt, unforgiveness.

Do you think it is really possible to "forget" the awful and traumatic events of our past?
No

Then what do you think Paul meant when he said to forget what is behind?
They must be dealt with by I John 1:9 and then removed from the focus of our lives. Until they are left at the foot of the cross, they remain in the forefront of our minds.

This could be a great time for people to share the things that keep them in bondage, allow the group to share appropriate scriptures, and then pray in faith so that each person can walk away from this experience by "forgetting what is behind."

What is the second step Paul says is necessary to move us forward toward the prize of the Lord?

Straining toward what is ahead

What is the Prize for which the Lord has called us heavenward?

That I may be conformed to the image of Christ (Romans 8:29). That I live under the blessing of the Lord as a testimony of the goodness of my God. That I can live a life of freedom.

Small Group Time

In your small group share with one another what God revealed to you in this study and what you are going to do about it. Pray for one another.

CPSIA information can be obtained
at www.ICGtesting.com
Printed in the USA
FFOW04n1901190915
17036FF